Staffing A Small Business: Hiring, Compensating, and Evaluating

by A.E. Worthington
& E.R. Worthington

Published by The Oasis Press

Grants Pass, Oregon

Published by The Oasis Press*
300 North Valley Drive
Grants Pass, Oregon 97526
503/479-9464

Copyright 1985, 1987 by A.E.Worthington & E.R.Worthington
All rights reserved.

Reproduction of this work, in whole or in part, without written permission of the publisher is prohibited. This book is offered for sale on the condition that its contents will be used by the purchaser or purchaser's agents and employees, for purchaser's personal use only. Anyone who reproduces any part of this book, or transfers any part of it, for unauthorized use will cause actual and material damage to the publisher and the authors.

International Standard Book Number - 0-916378-49-7

The publisher does not assume and hereby disclaims any liability to any party for any loss or damage caused by errors or omissions in **Staffing A Small Business: Hiring, Compensating, and Evaluating**, whether such errors or omissions result from negligence, accident or any other cause. Users of this book should modify the forms or substitute other provisions and language where, as will frequently be the case, the circumstances of a particular company situation require. The authors make no representation that the forms are suitable for all business circumstances and requirements.

Printed in the United States of America

10 9 8 7 6 5 4 3 2

*The Oasis Press is a registered trademark of
 Publishing Services, Inc. a Texas corporation,
 PSI Research in Oregon

Chapter 1
Introduction

Selecting people to fill company positions is no longer a simple process. Multiple changes have taken place requiring personnel selection and hiring to be subject to rules, regulations, human values, and market conditions which did not exist even a few years ago. Being unaware can easily lead to an unhappy match between employee and employer; at worst, a business owner can face lawsuits arising from illegal or discriminatory hiring or promotion practices. In today's world of litigation gratification, employers cannot afford to be ignorant in the personnel field.

This book is designed specifically for the small business owner and manager who is not a personnel specialist and for whose company having a personnel staff specialist is a luxury. The process of planning personnel needs for the future, establishing job positions that satisfy legal requirements, and advertising for and selecting good people is explained in straightforward, understandable language.

How to Use This Book

This book is designed to serve as a guide for a business that needs to hire a new employee. Each chapter addresses a specific aspect of the staffing process. At the beginning is a summary of what is included in that chapter to assist locating specific information. Reference sources are listed at the end of some chapters to help you locate more detailed information.

The staffing process may be divided into three phases.

o   Phase one involves the work required within the company to determine if another person (or position) is needed, and what must be done to fill the position. This phase mainly involves research to determine what is needed and how to get it within the established legal personnel framework.

o   Phase two is an active phase of seeking applicants, evaluating them, and selecting the best. This requires interpersonal skills and the ability to interact in a one-on-one interview. Again, knowledge of the legal structure is a needed asset.

o   Phase three is integrating the new employee into the work setting. A smooth transition generally results in a happy employee; ignoring the psychological shock of transition by letting a new employee sink or swim may lead to the loss of a valuable asset.

STAFFING A SMALL BUSINESS

This book may also be used for only part of the staffing process. If you already have a job description which is current and valid, and you only need to replace a vacancy, then those chapters pertaining to phase one may not be needed this time around.

Each chapter provides specific technical information on a particular step in the staffing process. Charts and worksheets are included to show how to set up policies and procedures in an organized, systematic process. These worksheets and blank forms may be reproduced only for internal use in staffing your business. Modify the forms as necessary to meet your needs.

The Staffing Process

There are 13 steps in the staffing processes' three phases. These cover all the tasks of determining what kind of additional (or different) personnel a business needs, locating and hiring them, and integrating them into the present work force. The steps are discussed below in more detail.

1. **Determining Work Requirements and Skills Needed**

    The first step in the staffing process is to look into the future of your company. Develop plans that describe the human resources needed to accomplish your goals. Knowing what expansion or changes are expected should lead to a recognition of which human resources and skills will be needed to staff this growth or change.

2. **Evaluating Present Staff**

    Compare the kinds of employees or skills you will need in the future with what is presently available in the company. Some of the present staff may already possess the necessary skills to occupy future positions. This human resource audit will allow you to quickly see who you may use from your present staff and what positions must be filled externally.

    Hiring someone new may be more or less expensive in terms of time and money than internal retraining or reorganizing.

3. **Describing the Job Position**

    Knowing that certain additional people are needed to occupy future jobs is one thing; formalizing the position by writing a job description is another. The written job description contains the title of the position, the supervisor, a narrative description of the job itself, the tasks to be performed, and the minimum requirements needed to successfully do the job.

4. **Establishing Job Requirements**

    The minimum requirements should be seriously considered. Federal law mandates that requirements cited as necessary for the job be relevant to

INTRODUCTION

the job and a requisite for job success. Compensation is also related to basic job requirements. Essentially, the task is to list the minimum acceptable skills and qualifications necessary to enter the position.

5. **Consider Legal Implications**

   The Civil Rights Act of 1964 and subsequent legislation has made the task of personnel management a profession in itself. Today, courts are making binding decisions regarding employee-employer relationships as well as determining the consequences if managers are ignorant of or choose to disregard court-sanctioned employee rights. Creating and filling job positions must be done with an appreciation of the underlying concepts of federal and state employment regulations.

6. **Determining Compensation**

   Compensation is more than an hourly wage or annual salary; it also refers to paid holidays, sick leave, health and disability insurance, death benefits, job security insurance, retirement, stock options, office location, cars provided, and more. The benefits may equal 20 to 35 percent of the actual cash paid. Hiring a $12,000-a-year secretary may, in fact, cost a business up to $16,000 annually. Compensation for a new position must be commensurate with that of similar existing positions, otherwise the groundwork will be laid for employee discontent, even civil court proceedings.

7. **Consider Union Implications**

   Unions serve as a strong voice for workers; over the years they have brought about increased wages, benefits, and improved working conditions for their members. Unions represent a cross section of jobs from industrial and manual workers to clerical and professional employees. Excessive demands can force a business into bankruptcy, as some major corporations have recently found.

8. **Look for Applicants**

   After setting down the job description, basic entry requirements, and ranges of compensation the quest for a person to fill the position begins. If your company lacks the necessary resource, outside soliciting takes place. Searching is easier if you know where and when to look for capable applicants. Know the right media to use in advertising a position: the local paper for finding a stock clerk, the Wall Street Journal to recruit an executive. Take advantage of local contacts such as your staff, suppliers, customers, and colleagues. State and private employment agencies, schools, and trade organizations are recruitment sources.

9. **Reviewing Applicants—The Selection Process**

   This step begins with the development of a good job application, in line with federal law, that enables the screener to quickly separate fully qualified applicants from the less qualified. Personal interviews are used to

STAFFING A SMALL BUSINESS

verbally verify the data on the application, to learn more about the applicant's job related skills, and to ascertain how the applicant responds during this interpersonal interaction. Objective guides, such as tests of skill or knowledge, should be used to evaluate prospective employees. After this, rank-order the applicants, assign a compensatory value on their worth, and offer the top rated applicant a position. If the person accepts, you have a new employee. If the applicant says "no," you go to your second choice and make another proposition.

10. **Hiring and Placing the New Employee**

    The new employee must fill out the myriad of federal, state, local, and company personnel forms. These constitute the beginning of the personnel record, with the first document being the completed job application.

    After completing the forms, the new hire is introduced to the company: orientation to benefits, business regulations and policies, work schedules, the work environment, and the supervisor and co-workers is in order. The new employee is now a part of your business.

11. **Career Progression**

    More and more people today do not want just a job—they want a career. More than a nine-to-five routine and annual cost of living and longevity increases, a career involves a systematic progression of increased responsibility, and increased rewards. The company that does not offer progressive career patterns eventually may lose its more aggressive employees and retain those who are less inclined to do more.

12. **Appraising Employee Performance**

    When compensation is tied to job performance, you must find the best way to uniformly evaluate the performance of everyone in spite of their dissimilar functions. New employees may be formally evaluated in 30, 60, and 90 days; regular employees may be formally evaluated every six to twelve months.

    Performance appraisals should not be secret. Strengths, as well as limitations, should be mentioned and a counseling session with the immediate supervisor should be held each time. The employee should be told what is needed to improve limited or unacceptable performance. In addition to the formal appraisals, informal feedback should be the rule, constantly letting employees know how valuable they are to the company or to point out areas where improvement or changes would be preferred.

INTRODUCTION

Moving Up or Out

Most employees eventually reach a point where they have gone as far as they can go in a particular job. Promotions, reassignments, transfers, retirements, or terminations are different ways to move someone up or out. In some cases neither the company nor the employee sees any reason for progressively increasing job responsibilities. In other instances, upward mobility is a vital method needed to open up new entry positions at the bottom. Policies in this area can have a large effect on budgets and on morale. Employers must judge their own situation and weigh the benefits and restrictions.

The staffing process can be one of the most costly expenses in terms of cash outlay and time invested. The human resources of a business are its most valuable assets. The staffing process should be conducted in a manner to ensure that your human assets will contribute to the value of your business, not detract from it.

Chart 1-1 is a checklist to help determine what your business lacks in the way of having an effective staffing process system. Each question answered in the negative suggests that work needs to be done in this area. The appropriate chapters where you can find help to develop that aspect of your business are also listed.

STAFFING A SMALL BUSINESS

Chart 1-1 Staffing Process Checklist with References

	Chapter Reference
1. Have I determined what new or different job requirements will be needed in the next six to twelve months?	2, 3
2. Have I determined what new or different people skills will be needed in the next six to twelve months?	2, 3
3. Are there any people on my present staff who have the needed skills?	3, 4, 11, 12, 14
4. Are there any people on my present staff who have the potential to be trained to acquire new skills?	3, 4, 11, 12, 14
5. Can I afford to train any potential current employees?	3, 4, 12, 14
6. Do I have a written description of the new job position?	4
7. Have I determined what the minimal acceptable requirements are for a person to fill the position?	4, 5
8. What laws (if any) apply to the job position?	5
9. What should I pay the person (to include all benefits)?	6
10. Are unions involved? If so, how?	7
11. Where is the most effective place to find the right person to fill the position?	4, 8
12. Do I have a process developed to review all applicants the same way?	8, 9
13. Do I know what I need to know to select the best applicant?	4, 5, 6, 9
14. What if the applicant I select does not want the job?	9
15. Do I have a formal company orientation process to effectively place the new hire on my staff?	10
16. Do I have a good personnel records system?	11
17. Does my company have a well defined career progression system?	3, 4, 6, 10, 12
18. Does my company have a formal employee performance appraisal procedure?	12
19. Does my company have a formal process for promoting employees—or terminating unsatisfactory performers?	11, 12, 13
20. Does my company have any formalized staff training and development programs?	14

Chapter 2
Defining Your Business
(Where Are You Now)

Summary of Chapter

Defining the status of your business is an adjunct part of the staffing process. Strategic planning for future needs presumes that the business at present has a well-defined purpose, that goals and objectives are clearly understood by everyone, and that strategies have been developed to achieve the stated goals. If confusion exists regarding the present status of a business, projections for the future will most likely be confused, too.

This chapter contains a brief explanation of strategic planning. Worksheets are included to allow you to write your plans for each phase relative to your business. Many small business owners have most of this in their heads. Writing it down makes future planning easier because you are constantly referring back to the same basic information. Filing it only in your head continually leaves the plans, your basic reference data, subject to change.

Purpose

Purpose, as described in this section, refers to the reason for being in business (aside from making money). The statement of purpose should clearly define what your business does that makes it different from other businesses in the same industry.

Restaurants prepare and serve food to customers. A general purpose statement of a restaurant owner might be: "To own and operate a fast food restaurant specializing in Chinese foods catering primarily to lunch and dinner crowds."

This purpose statement is short, simple, and to the point. It states the activities the business performs and who the customers are. Purpose statements should be based on strong market research to ensure that the intended business purpose does, in fact, match an unmet need.

A part of the purpose statement may include the business philosophy and beliefs of the owner. These are the guidelines for the manner in which the business is conducted. These beliefs specify how you intend to interact with the clientele you will serve. They may include your concepts of trust, honesty, service, quality, volume, price, value, and so on.

STAFFING A SMALL BUSINESS

The purpose statement may be as long or as short as you want. The important point to remember is that a purpose statement should clearly state what the business is created to do and what activities the business will perform. Your personal beliefs on how to operate the business may also be included.

Goals and Objectives

These two words may be used to mean the same thing, namely, what results you expect to achieve. Goals may be stipulated as short-term (usually within your fiscal year) or long-term (extending beyond your fiscal year into the future). Goals or objectives must fall into three areas if they are to have any value to the business.

First, a goal must be objectively measurable; that is, the goal must be defined in such a way that anyone will know when it has been reached. Goals like "to increase sales," "be nicer to our customers," or "cut our expenses" are not clearly measurable. They do not state how much. The goals could be stated "to increase sales ten percent over last year," or "to be nicer to our customers by having an annual customer appreciation sale," or "to cut our expenses by 10 percent from what we spent last year."

Second, a goal must have a specific time or date of completion. To increase sales by 10 percent or to reduce expenses by 10 percent is measurable, but when do you take the measurement? "Our goal for this fiscal year is to increase total sales by 10 percent from January through June as compared with the total sales of last July through December." This goal clearly states that the comparison is total sales from one six-month period against a previous six-month period. Not only is this goal measurable, but you know when to do the measuring.

The third rule is that the goal must be realistic. Goals that are not attainable tend to frustrate employees and generate dissatisfaction; goals that are beyond the reasonable reach of a business are not seen as worth striving for. As a result, an attainable standard is lacking and employees lose a sense of commitment and direction.

Do your goals meet these criteria?

Strategies and Plans

Strategies are plans. Business strategies are those plans developed to allow the business to achieve its goals. If the goal was to save enough money in the next fiscal year to add a new wing to your office, then the strategy would be the method or methods selected to save the money.

DEFINING YOUR BUSINESS

Worksheet 2-1 The Purpose of the Business

1. What do you intend to do?   or
   What are you doing?

2. What is your intended market?   or
   What is your actual market?

3. What is your business philosophy?

STAFFING A SMALL BUSINESS

Worksheet 2-2 Goals and Objectives

1. Are they measurable?

2. Have you established a time frame by which they must be accomplished?

3. Are they reasonable and attainable?

DEFINING YOUR BUSINESS

In most cases, once a goal has been selected, several possible ways to achieve it are considered. As each one is evaluated, it may be rejected or set aside as a possibility. This process should finally yield the best method (plan or strategy) to accomplish the goal. Businesses may have a major strategy (saving money) that will be attained by using several minor strategies (reduce spending in specific areas, reduce outstanding credit, become more aggressive regarding collecting past due accounts, take advantage of vendor discounts).

Strategies or plans are the specific ways you intend to conduct your business over time (usually within a fiscal year, perhaps broken down by quarter) to achieve the goals you have established.

Policies

The guidelines developed to run the business on a day-to-day basis are company policies. Policies refer to the routine, ordinary functions that occur all the time to keep the business going. Policies may be established regarding duties, lunch breaks, customer interactions, dress code, or standards of performance.

Small businesses, often referred to as *Mom-and-Pop* operations, may have most of their policies in a very informal form, and the operating rules may be mostly passed on verbally. As the size of the company increases or the business becomes more complex, written policies are a more efficient way of ensuring that all employees have the same understanding of the company policies.

Today, many businesses have an employee handbook or a company policy manual, a current document indicating what is expected in all routine operations of the business and what specific performance or behaviors are restricted, limited or prohibited. A company policy manual assists management in making people decisions and provides the workers the opportunity to see what they should do, what they can do, and what they cannot do.

A policy manual enhances organizational communication, simplifies decision making, and decreases frustration because written guidelines increase the probability that employees will be treated consistently in similar situations.

Structures

Structure refers to how the organizational resources are arranged to carry out the operations of the company. In most businesses the structure is like a pyramid, as shown in Chart 2-1. The lowest level, the base, is wide because it is the worker level. As the levels of responsibility increase, the number of subordinates each manager supervises decreases.

When designing the structure, a major principle should be kept in mind: each person should report only to one boss. All persons should also know where they fit within the organization.

STAFFING A SMALL BUSINESS

The structure is arranged to achieve certain ends. Because of this, the primary concern should be to organize employees in the manner which will most effectively make the strategies work.

If the tasks to be performed by employees are typical in scope and complexity, the standard pyramid structure should suffice. If the tasks are relatively simple and repetitive (digging a ditch, filling orders, stocking shelves), a short and wide structure may be suitable. This consists of many workers, but few supervisors or managers.

On the other hand, if the job requirements are not routine but very complex, demanding considerable supervision, the tall and narrow structure may be best. This requires more supervisors with fewer workers to control than the other structure.

The design selected to organize your human resources should be based on:

o The tasks performed

o The goals to be achieved

o The strategies selected to reach those goals

Employees

Employees are the backbone and the fiber of any business. They have both a value to a company and, by their efforts, create the value of a business.

It is incumbent on management to make every possible effort to select the right people for the right job. This takes considerable time and effort, if done correctly. Know what you need and provide the right compensation to hire those you need.

The job does not end with the hiring. Continue to upgrade the skills of your employees and reward them accordingly. If you don't provide rewards for employees, chances are they won't extend themselves for your business.

Constraints and Limitations

All businesses operate within internal and external environments, which may affect the business in either a positive or negative manner.

The internal environment includes the company's purpose, goals, plans, policies, structure, and the people from the boss to the lowest paid worker. It also includes the interactions of these factors. The potential of a business may be limited by management skills and the quality of employees, or these same factors may become the difference between an average and an outstanding company.

DEFINING YOUR BUSINESS

Worksheet 2-3 Strategies and Plans

1. List possible alternatives and options.

2. List the advantages and disadvantages of each one.

3. Select the best plan or the best combination to achieve your goals.

STAFFING A SMALL BUSINESS

Worksheet 2-4 Company Policies

1. Are your policies in any written form?

2. Do you have a company policy manual?

3. Do you have a company employee handbook?

4. What are the most frequent questions asked regarding company policies?

   o Vacation

   o Sick leave

   o Insurance

   o Termination

   o Overtime

   o Promotions

   o Pay raises

   o Holidays

   o Profit sharing

   o Travel

   o Educational assistance

   o Smoking

   o Grievance procedures

   o Other

Which of the above policies are written and available to all employees?

DEFINING YOUR BUSINESS

Chart 2-1 Organizational Structures

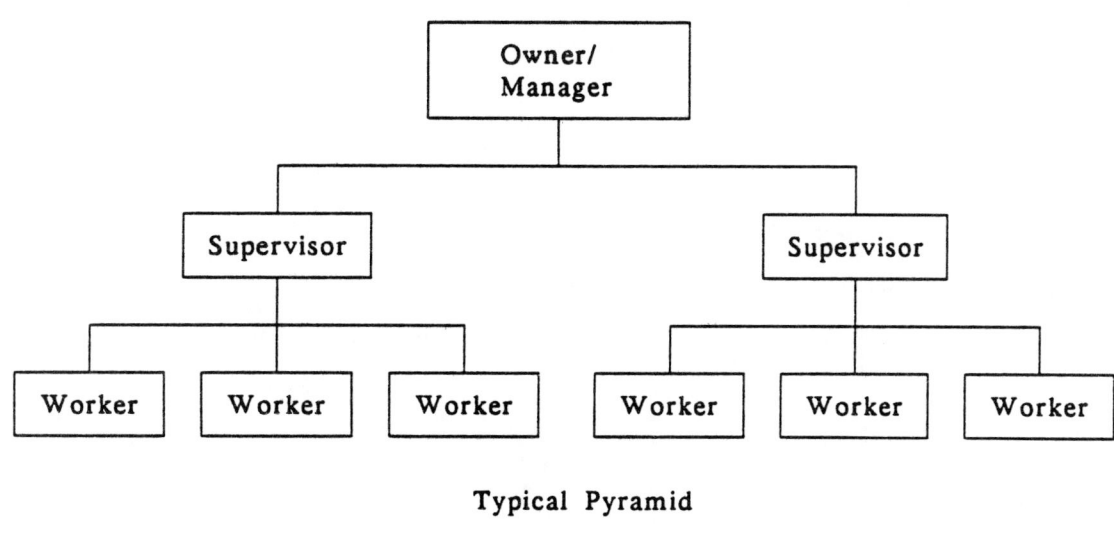

Typical Pyramid

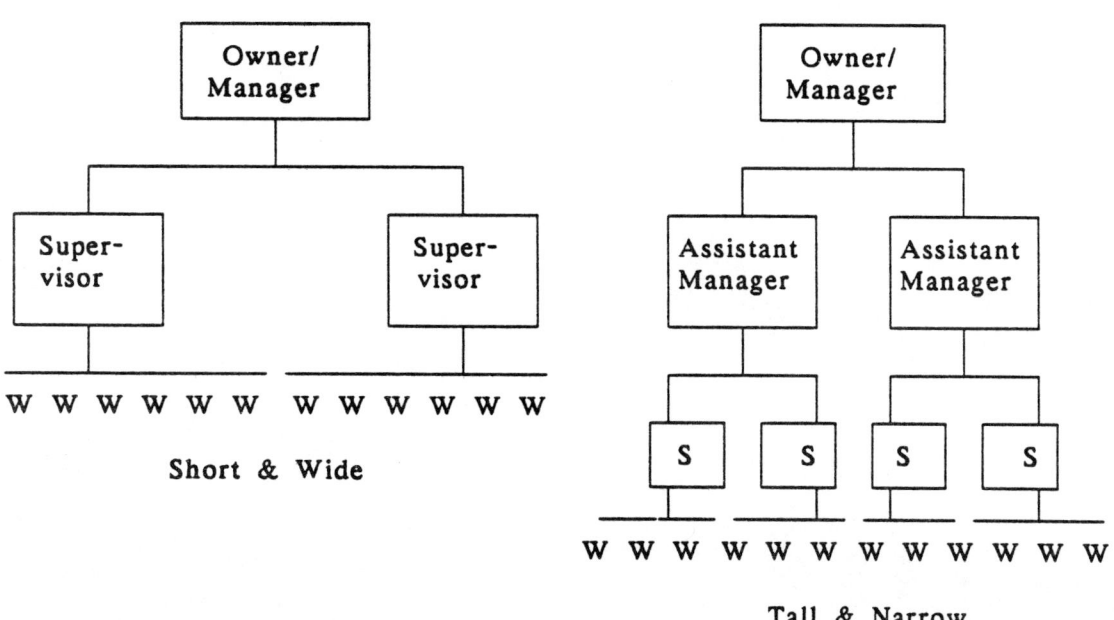

Short & Wide

Tall & Narrow

STAFFING A SMALL BUSINESS

Worksheet 2-5 Organizational Structure

Draw an organization chart that represents your company.

DEFINING YOUR BUSINESS

The external environment consists of everything outside the company, those factors or people over which the company has no direct control. Examples of the external environment may be customers, suppliers, competitors, neighbors, or any level of government.

Business people must be aware of both the internal and external environments and the effect they may have on the business. It is imperative that you know which factors may affect your ongoing operations and planning, directly or indirectly.

Most business people are normally cognizant of the internal environment, since they create and manage it. The external environment may not be as visible. The factors that may affect business operations usually fall into the general categories of environmental, economic, legal, and social-cultural.

Environmental factors may be chemical, air or noise pollution, or laws that affect what you want to do. Land use, zoning, and traffic restraints are other examples. Local concerned citizens may band together to oppose or promote your plans regarding business expansion or extended working hours.

Economic factors typically relate to values placed on goods or services; the standard of living; depression, recession, or inflation; the cost of money, labor, or raw materials; and, of course, the laws of supply and demand.

Legal factors refer to laws, regulations, and rules which affect your business. These may be burdensome; on the other hand, legal factors may favor your operations with reduced taxes, trade protection, government loans, or other forms of legislation.

Social and cultural factors may work in mysterious ways. The values, customs, biases, beliefs, and whims of humans may work for or against the business, seemingly without reason.

SLOT Analysis

Planning for the future should recognize which factors may enhance or constrain desired operations. One way to help sort out the factors and understand how they will affect future operations is to do a SLOT analysis. SLOT stands for Strengths, Limitations, Opportunities, and Threats. Strengths and limitations refer to factors in the internal environment relative to planning. Opportunities and threats refer to factors in the external environment related to planning.

If expansion plans for a business were being developed, the availability of a qualified labor pool would be a strength while the lack of it would become a limitation. The introduction of a local manufacturing firm into a town becomes an opportunity for many businesses which would service the community but a threat to an existing firm in the same business.

STAFFING A SMALL BUSINESS

A way to use the SLOT analysis is to list all of the internal and external factors you are aware of and then assign an S, L, O, or T to each one. A preponderance of S's or O's encourages you to proceed with your planning. A majority of L's and T's suggests that objectives may not be reached, and the business might be better off if the planning went in a different direction.

The SLOT analysis worksheet should help you list and categorize all of the factors affecting your planning, and recognize whether the impact will be positive or negative. Chart 2-2 gives a concrete example of a SLOT analysis.

References

1. **Develop Your Business Plan.** Richard L. Leza and Jose F. Placencia. Oasis Press, 720 S. Hillview Drive, Milpitas, CA, 95035, 1984.

2. **A Company Policy and Personnel Workbook.** Ardella R. Ramey and Ronald A. Mrozek. Oasis Press, 720 S. Hillview Dr., Milpitas, CA 95035, 1985.

DEFINING YOUR BUSINESS

Chart 2-2 SLOT Analysis

Situation: A local publishing company is considering writing and publishing a four-page, non-denominational Christian newsletter once a month to sell to local churches for inclusion in their monthly church bulletins.

Internal Environment	S	L
Purpose: Use existing personnel and facilities to publish another newsletter aimed at local churches	X	
Goals/Objectives: Increase revenues 15% in one year by focusing on a new market	X	
Strategies: Use existing publishing concepts and marketing strategies to sell newsletter. Presently no one is doing this.	X	
Company Policies: Not applicable	N/A	N/A
Organizational Structure: Equipment and personnel are available to publish the newsletter	X	
Employees: All employees are available except a writer	X	

External Environment	O	T
Environmental: Not applicable	N/A	N/A
Economic: Local churches might have some finnancial concerns which would affect sales		X
Legal: Not applicable	N/A	N/A
Social & Cultural: To be cost effective, all subscribers would receive the same materials. This might result in the contents being too general for universal acceptance by all churches.		X
Conclusions: Two problems must be overcome: (1) obtaining a qualified part-time writer and (2) ensuring that the materials would have universal appeal.		

Chapter 3
Human Resource Forecast Planning
(Where You Want to Be)

Summary of Chapter

The chapter presents how a business uses its plans for the future to forecast what kind and how many workers will be needed in the years to come. This issue should be of concern because the business may expand, contract, or change what it does. Any one of these changes will require the owner or manager to make decisions regarding current employees. Whether to promote current employees into new positions or leave them in their present jobs and hire new outside employees may be a difficult choice. Unplanned changes can create a dissatisfied work force. Planned changes allow for decreasing or expanding the work force in an orderly manner. Forecasting is only part of the job. When future needs are determined, an analysis of the current employees and the external labor pool is required to decide where the new employees will come from.

Predicting Future Needs

Forecasting is a process of determining how many people will be needed to run the business in the future.

Forecasting begins with an understanding of where the business wants to be in the future. If growth is planned in the current business, then the major concern may be how to increase the present work force with the same type of employees. If the growth is through geographical expansion, such as opening a branch in another location, then the need for employees may not be to increase the number of workers but rather to duplicate the staff from the manager on down.

Entirely new staff requirements may be needed if the business expands into a new industry or technology. Converting from manual typewriters to word processors or from hand-filled ledgers to computerized accounting systems may require skills not held by present employees.

Chart 3-1 is an example of how change in a business can require changes in personnel and may necessitate an organizational change. Recognizing where personnel changes will occur in the organization leads to a better understanding of the additional employee skills that are needed.

STAFFING A SMALL BUSINESS

Chart 3-1 Predicting Future Needs

Current Organizational Structure

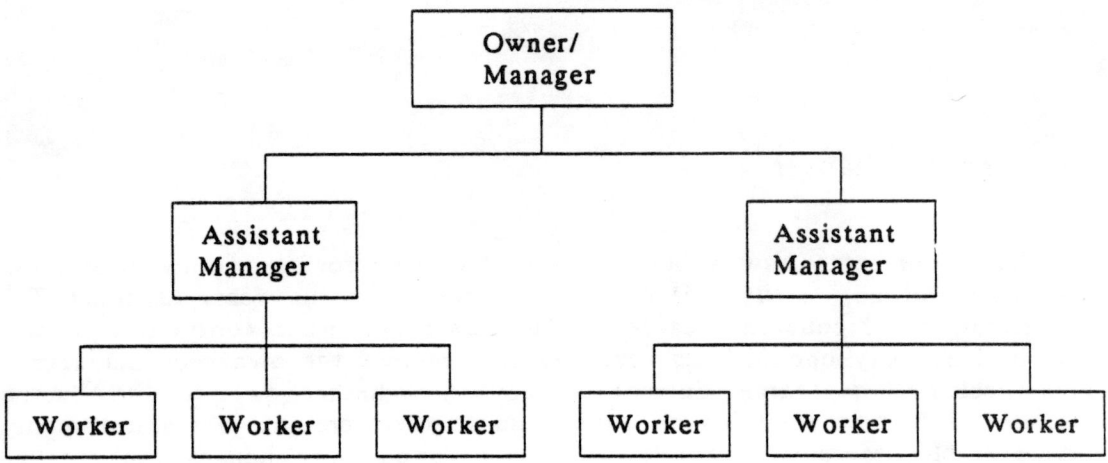

Changes to be made next year: Add a third shift to operations to increase productivity 35 percent.

Personnel changes required: A third shift will require a third assistant manager and three new workers.

New Organizational Structure

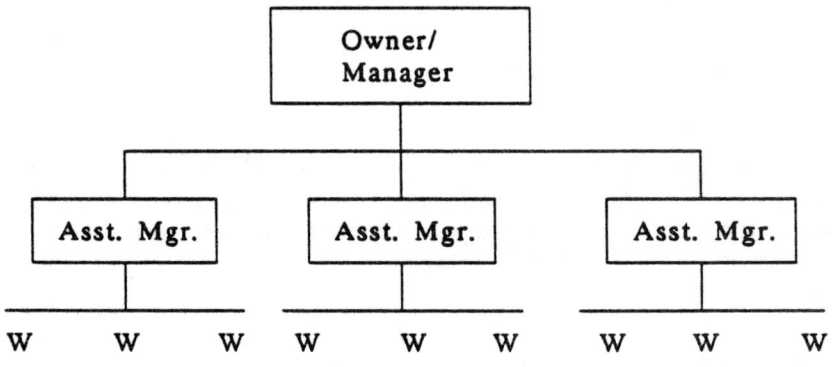

HUMAN RESOURCE FORECAST PLANNING

Establishing Staffing Requirements

Future staffing requirements are based on the predicted changes that will occur in an organization over a specific time period. Planning changes in a business to include staff revisions helps to determine exactly which skills will be needed and at what level within the organization.

Several different aspects of human resource planning must be considered to project staffing requirements. Chart 3-2 lists what should be considered when determining if additional employees will be needed. The order presented is not the only way to prioritize these considerations.

New position requirements should be developed as low as possible within the business structure. It is usually easier to expand the responsibilities of a position than to contract them. In many cases positions are filled by people who have the experience and qualifications to assume more responsibility in the future. An understanding is reached between employee and employer that increased success of the business can lead to further job expansion and growth. As growth occurs, the duties of the new position can also expand and grow. On the other hand, it can be expensive to hire a highly qualified person for a position that currently requires only minimal preparation. When planning future staff positions, try to determine if the position will change little or if it will grow.

When the general staffing requirements have been outlined for the new position, the next step, an internal human resource audit, can begin.

Human Resource Audit (Internal)

An internal human resource audit is an evaluation of current employees to see if any are capable of and want to fill any new positions.

The person responsible for staffing must have access to the background, experience, qualifications, potential, and desire for promotions of every employee. (Refer to Chapters 11, 12, and 14 for more information about setting up a personnel file where this information should be maintained.) The skills and performance of each employee are evaluated to determine the employee's suitability for any new position. No one with potential should be overlooked.

A management promotion potential chart like Chart 3-3 should be maintained on all employees that are considered as potential replacements for management positions. The chart lists the management position with the names of those employees that may be potential replacements for that position. An employee may be considered as a potential management candidate for various positions, not necessarily just the area they work in.

The new position promotional potential chart lists candidates who can be considered for new positions (see Chart 3-4). This chart describes the new position and then lists those employees who are eligible for consideration for the new position.

STAFFING A SMALL BUSINESS

Chart 3-2 Staffing Requirement Considerations

1. What are the general functions needed in this position (i.e., what will the person be doing)?

2. Is the position temporary or permanent?

3. Is the position full-time or part-time?

4. Is the position a supervisory or managerial position?

5. What will the position cost the business (salary, benefits, etc.)?

6. Does the expected increase in productivity justify the cost of the position?

7. Are there any special skills or qualifications required that are not typically associated with this type of position?

8. Who will the person filling the position report to?

9. Does the position have career potential or is it a closed-end position?

10. What effect will this new position have on similar positions already occupied in the business?

11. Can the duties of this position be assumed by any other positions in the business or is it necessary to create this new position?

HUMAN RESOURCE FORECAST PLANNING

Chart 3-3 Management Promotion Potential Chart

Legend		
Name		Performance Rating
Position	Years with Business	Promotion Rating

General Manager

Smith, J.		1
Asst. Mgr.	15	1
Jones, S.		1
Asst. Mgr.	2	2

Assistant Manager			Assistant Manager		
Brown, C.		1	Munoz, J.		1
Sr. Sales Clerk	3	1	Sr. Sales Clerk	4	1
Perez, W.		1	Watson, L.		2
Sr. Sales Clerk	4	1	Weekend Mgr.	5	2
Long, A.		2	Shelly, T.		1
Sr. Sales Clerk	7	2	Sales Clerk	2	3
Watson, L.		2	Long, A.		2
Weekend Mgr.	5	2	Sr. Sales Clerk	7	2

Performance Rating

1. Outstanding
2. Average
3. Needs improvement
4. Poor

Promotion Rating

1. Promotable now
2. Needs some training
3. Needs considerable training
4. Not considered at this time
5. Does not desire promotion

STAFFING A SMALL BUSINESS

Chart 3-4 New Position Promotional Potential

New Position: Senior Sales Clerk
Responsible for supervising men's clothing department sales clerks, cash and charge sales accountability, and replacing stock on shelves and racks.

Eligible Employees

Name: Ralph Jones	Performance Rating
Position: Sales Clerk, Men's Wear	2
	Promotion Rating
Years with business: 3	1
Name: Sally Smith	Performance Rating
Position: Sales Clerk, Men's Wear	1
	Promotion Rating
Years with business: 1	2
Name: Judy Brown	Performance Rating
Position: Senior Sales Clerk, Infants	2
	Promotion Rating
Years with business: 10	1

Performance Rating	Promotion Rating
1. Outstanding	1. Promotable now
2. Average	2. Needs some training
3. Needs improvement	3. Needs considerable training
4. Poor	4. Not considered at this time
	5. Does not desire promotion

Note that both charts list two different ratings or grades. The first rating is a summary of past performance, defined by one of four categories: outstanding, average, needs improvement, or poor. These should be the same ratings used on the employee performance appraisal form.

The second rating is an evaluation of the employee's promotion potential, based on whatever factors the manager deems important or relevant. This rating has five categories: promotable now, needs some training, needs considerable training, not considered at this time, and does not desire promotion. This last category allows the manager to rank someone deemed capable of being a manager, yet notes that the person does not want to be promoted.

Upgrading Employees

Upward mobility is a good way to retain excellent employees. If a business creates new positions, current employees may want to move up into them. If highly motivated employees have managerial potential but lack some technical skills necessary for success, the staffing manager should consider the cost (in terms of money and employee satisfaction) of training them for the position versus filling the position from outside.

Chart 3-5 demonstrates a method to determine which employee skills need upgrading and the costs of upgrading them. The chart specifies the exact nature of the training and cost in time and money.

Hiring New Employees

Filling a position from outside the company can become a frustrating task if the employer does not know exactly what is needed or the availability of the labor supply. The higher the qualifications for the job, the harder it may be to find the right person. If the skills required are minimal, most likely there will always be applicants available; such positions, though, do not always offer upward career movement. Workers at all levels tend to come and go unless some type of career progression is built into a position.

As the demand for skill requirements and prior experience increases, applicants tend to be interested in the quality of the position and the business environment as well as the salary. This clearly suggests that positions being developed today must not only meet the needs of the organization, they must also meet the needs of the employee.

In a market where the labor pool exceeds the supply of jobs, finding qualified people may not be difficult; keeping them if they are good employees may be another matter. Good employees almost always find work, regardless of the job market conditions. When the job supply exceeds the demand, it is even more crucial to offer a position that presents a career opportunity within the organization.

STAFFING A SMALL BUSINESS

Chart 3-5 Employee Training Assessment Chart

Employee Name	JONES, Peter	WILLIAMS, Anita	SANDS Janet	ROBERTS Sam	JETT Bob
Current Position	Assistant Manager Production	Secretary	Clerk	Shipping Clerk	Salesman
Desired Position	Manager Sales	Secretarial Supervisor	Bookkeeper	Assistant Stocking Supervisor	Manager Sales
Skills/ Experience Required	Experience managing sales people	Familiarity with all office equipment	Advanced bookkeeping techniques	Inventory and stocking techniques	Experience managing sales people
Skills lacking	Familiarity with sales procedures	Experience with computers	Advanced bookkeeping experience	Inventory techniques	Experience managing people
Training Available	On-the-job training with sales manager	City college computer course	Junior college advanced bookkeeping	Small Business Administration inventory course	On-the-job assignment as assistant to manager
Time Required	one month	eight weeks	one semester three-hour course	one week	Six months
Cost	none	$500	$160	$75	none

Chart 3-6 illustrates an example of a career progression plan for a sales trainee in a home appliance retail store. One year of on-the-job training leads to a sales clerk position, and after two more successful years, a supervisory sales clerk position. This, in turn, with the required formal educational background, can lead to an assistant manager position in two more years.

Opportunities for advancement should be part of any position being offered to the public. Positions without upward progression either tend to attract marginally qualified people or are viewed by employees as temporary jobs, to be dropped for something better.

Analysis of the Labor Market

Planning for the future of your business requires both a knowledge of your business and knowledge of the availability of labor to fill your positions.

Several trends for the next fifteen years must be recognized when developing career-progressive positions. More people continue working beyond the ages of 60 to 65. The baby boom generation will mean a much larger percentage of the population in the 40-to-65 age group. These factors, plus the increase of female and minority managers, mean that the labor supply for mid to upper-level management positions will exceed demand.

Many managers today are not computer literate; they have not grown up with the personal computer. Today's elementary students are acquiring computer skills from the first grade on. Tomorrow's high school students will graduate with computer skills as common as reading, writing and math.

Managers must also know what other capabilities the high school and college graduates have when they enter the work force. Skills the job candidates have must match the skills needed in new positions. If new graduates do not have the required background, then perhaps someone else's employees must be considered. For example, experienced accountants do not come out of business schools, they come from accounting firms or accounting departments of other businesses.

Before a business develops a new position, it must ensure that there are skilled people available to fill that position at a cost the business can afford. Positions for which candidates are too rare or too costly may be worse than not having the position to begin with. Avoid developing positions that cannot be filled.

STAFFING A SMALL BUSINESS

Chart 3-6 Career Progression Chart

	Position Description	Job Requirements	Career Opportunities
Entry Position	Title: Sales Trainee. Entry level position in home appliance retail business. Supervised by regular sales clerk.	High school diploma. Ability to meet people. Ability to sell a product.	Upward progression in sales area, into sales management marketing, or marketing operations.
1 Year Post Entry	Title: Sales Clerk. Show and demonstrate appliance products to customers. Conclude cash or charge sales.	High school diploma. Minimum of one year sales experience; at least two months in appliance area. Knowledge of products.	Upward progression in sales area, into sales management, marketing, or retail operations.
3 Years Post Entry	Title: Senior Sales Clerk. Supervise sales clerks. Show and demonstrate appliance products. Conclude cash or charge sales. Institute credit checks.	College courses in sales and marketing. Attended advanced manufacturer's sales course. Experience training new sales people. Knowledge of products.	Progression into sales, marketing retail or wholesale operations as assistant manager or manager.
5 Years Post Entry	Title: Assistant Store Manager. Assist store manager in all aspects of conducting retail operations of store.	Two year college degree in sales, marketing, management, or business experience as senior sales clerk. Demonstrated management potential. Knowledge of products.	Progression into store manager position or department manager of retail, wholesale or marketing operations.

HUMAN RESOURCE FORECAST PLANNING

Worksheet 3-1 Predicting Future Needs

Your Current Organizational Structure

Changes to be made in the next year:

Personnel changes required:

New Organizational Structure

STAFFING A SMALL BUSINESS

Worksheet 3-2 Management Promotional Potential Chart

List your organization management positions here

Legend	
Name:	Performance Rating
Position:	
Age:	Promotion Rating
Years with business:	

Performance Rating	Promotion Rating
1. Outstanding 2. Average 3. Needs improvement 4. Poor	1. Promotable now 2. Needs some training 3. Needs considerable training 4. Not considered at this time 5. Does not desire promotion

HUMAN RESOURCE FORECAST PLANNING

Worksheet 3-3 New Position Promotional Potential

New Position:

Eligible Employees

Name: Performance Rating

Position:

                                        Promotion Rating

Years with business:

Name: Performance Rating

Position:

                                        Promotion Rating

Years with business:

Name: Performance Rating

Position:

                                        Promotion Rating

Years with business:

Name: Performance Rating

Position:

                                        Promotion Rating

Years with business:

Performance Rating	Promotion Rating
1. Outstanding	1. Promotable now
2. Average	2. Needs some training
3. Needs improvement	3. Needs considerable training
4. Poor	4. Not considered at this time
	5. Does not desire promotion

STAFFING A SMALL BUSINESS

Worksheet 3-4 Employee Training Assessment Chart

Employee Name			
Current Position			
Desired Position			
Skills/ Experience Required			
Skills Lacking			
Training Available			
Time Required			
Cost			

HUMAN RESOURCE FORECAST PLANNING

Worksheet 3-5 Career Progression Plan

	Position Description	Job Requirements	Career Opportunities
Entry Position	Title:		
___Year Post Entry	Title:		
___Years Post Entry	Title:		
___Years Post Entry	Title:		

Chapter 4

Human Resource Recruitment Planning

Summary of Chapter

The workload of an organization is usually divided into job functions; these are further divided into positions. The job positions separate work responsibilities and make it possible for employees to know the specific tasks they perform within the company. Job positions, then, are one way to distinguish one employee's job duties from another's.

The establishment of a job position is a part of the company's organizing process. Defining a particular job considers the tasks performed by an employee in the position and sets the minimum qualifications necessary for adequate performance of the job duties.

This chapter explains how to develop a job analysis and how to write the job description. The job description is used to recruit for the position. It can also be used as a standard to compare the actual job performance against. Sources for recruiting are presented and discussed.

Introduction

Human resource recruitment planning is establishing, in advance, a standard of job requirements that can be used to compare applicants. This standard sets the minimum levels required for adequate performance of the tasks that make up the job duties.

Before discussing this subject in detail, it will be helpful to know a few terms:

TASK: A definite work activity with a beginning and an end: "Answer phone and direct calls to recipients or take messages."

DUTY: Several related tasks: "Serve as receptionist for office; answer phone, greet visitors, give information and directions, take messages and deliver them to appropriate person."

POSITION: The tasks and duties performed by one person; title used to distinguish one employee's duties from another. For example, a receptionist position involves answering phone calls, giving information, and routine clerical work.

STAFFING A SMALL BUSINESS

JOB: One or more positions in the organization; more than one person may work in the same position and employees in the same position may work at different payroll levels.

JOB FAMILY: Several similar jobs. These may be in one office or may be spread throughout the organization.

JOB ANALYSIS: Study of job content that lists the work performed by tasks, duties, and responsibilities.

JOB DESCRIPTION: A written outline or summary of the work performed listing the tasks, duties, and responsibilities.

JOB SPECIFICATION: A written outline that lists the minimal skills, education, and experience necessary for a person to perform the job.

Job Analysis

Prior to hiring a person, there should be a written job description. Before writing this, a job analysis should be conducted. This is a systematic process used to develop a description of the job. A job analysis can be conducted either on a position not yet defined or on a current position.

Job analysis begins with collecting information on individual job positions indicating major duties and responsibilities assigned by supervisors.

For a current position occupied by an employee with no job description, the job analysis can begin with the person in the job completing a job sheet (Chart 4-1). It is used to help complete the job analysis form to record the information needed to write a job description.

Positions are classified as full-time, part-time, or temporary as follows:

o **Full-time:** employment is continuous, pay is based on a forty-hour work week (or the standard workweek of the company), and the jobholder is eligible to participate in the company's benefit programs.

o **Part-time:** Employment is continuous, normal workweek is less than the standard workweek. Part-time employees are generally not included in the company's benefit programs.

o **Temporary:** period of employment is less than three months or otherwise specified for a definite short period. Temporary help can be full-time or part-time but have no benefit rights.

Another aspect of employee classifications is that of exemptions. Some employees are exempt from minimum wage or overtime provisions, including; executive, administrative, and professional employees, and outside salespeople.

Employees of some small retail or service enterprises, seasonal recreational facilities, small newspapers, small telephone company operators, seamen on foreign vessels, fishermen, certain farm workers, and casual babysitters or companions to elderly may also be exempt. For more specific details refer to the Fair Labor Standards Act or contact the local Wage-Hour Administration Office.

For example, in most states a person trained and licensed as a psychology associate is limited in what he or she can do and must be supervised by a person licensed as a psychologist in that state. The person conducting the job analysis must be aware of the legal limitations and supervisory requirements of a psychology associate.

A job analysis should concentrate on what the position is being designed to accomplish. Do not confuse the job to be done with the person in the job or the concept of the "right" person for the job. Develop the analysis purely on what the functions are to be.

Concentrate on creating a position in which the functions are of a similar nature. Rather than expand the functions to create a full-time position, recognize if the requirements of the job do not call for the standard workweek. Develop the analysis in a logical work-related fashion. Do not add tasks just to fill a regular work routine.

The completed job analysis form is used to develop the job description. The job analysis form has two major sections: Part A—Requirements of the job, and Part B—Requirements of the employee.

Part A begins with a brief explanation of the purpose and nature of the job. Next is a general list of the work to be done, then a list of the tasks the job calls for. Additional information is needed regarding the tools required to perform the tasks; how much supervision is received; and who the person in the position supervises. The last part lists information about the personal contacts necessary to accomplish the tasks. All of this information pertains to the functions of the job.

Part B lists the qualifications needed to successfully perform the listed tasks. The section begins with a list of the formal training and educational requirements, starting with general education and leading into specific vocational, apprentice, or licensing training. It is followed by aptitudes and personality traits necessary to function satisfactorily in this position. Physical demands required by the position, as well as the conditions encountered in the work situation, are clearly defined. Lastly, licenses, certifications or other registry requirements necessary to legally serve in the position are listed.

The job analysis is a lengthy, detailed form which clearly describes and defines all aspects of a position. The information in this document is the basis for writing the job description. Chart 4-2 shows an example.

Some important points should be addressed when conducting a job analysis. Whoever is conducting the analysis must have a basic knowledge of the job

STAFFING A SMALL BUSINESS

Chart 4-1 Job Sheet

Department: <u>Administrative Office</u>

1. What is your job called?

    Secretary-receptionist

2. Who is your **immediate** senior and what is his or her job called?

    Mrs. Tanner — Office Manager

3. If you have **immediate** juniors, what are their jobs called?

    I have none.

4. What tasks do you carry out? (List duties in order of importance and after each task estimate percentage of time spent on the task).

    Answer the phone and direct calls to the appropriate person in the office.—50%

    Greet visitors to the office and assist them.—20%

    Type letters and files as requested by Mrs. Tanner.—15%

    Collect incoming mail and distribute.—5%

    File correspondence, memos, and other data.—5%

    Other routine office duties, mainly helping other people sort, collate or file materials.—5%

Signature   R. A. Tanner   Date   June 5, 1987

HUMAN RESOURCE RECRUITMENT PLANNING

Chart 4-2 Job Analysis

A job analysis is an evaluation of the duties and responsibilities of a job. It details what a worker does, how, why, and the circumstances under which it is done. The information collected from this job analysis will be used to develop a job description for various job positions.

Job Title __Electronic Technician__   Department __Maintenance__

Employment Classification __Full-time permanent position__

Part A. Requirements of the job.

1. **Job Summary** (A brief statement covering purpose and nature of the job):

   Installs and repairs electronic equipment and components in production line machinery. Inspects electronic equipment on preventive maintenance schedule. Maintains file of machinery electronic specifications, wiring diagrams, and blueprints.

2. **Work performed:**

   A. Installs electronic equipment following blueprints and manufacturer's specifications using hand tools and test equipment.

   B. Diagnoses electrical malfunctions by investigating reported symptoms and examining equipment using test instruments and wiring diagrams.

   C. Repairs electronic equipment to meet original specifications using test equipment and hand tools.

3. **Description of tasks:**

   A. Provides on-line service for production equipment to restore its proper function if it breaks down.

   B. Inspects electronic equipment on preventive maintenance schedule to ensure that it is operating at optimum level. Maintains file of machinery specifications, wiring diagrams, and blueprints.

   C. Records repair and/or maintenance work on work order form daily and forwards it to maintenance supervisor at end of work shift.

   D. Keeps repair and maintenance logs on electronic equipment. When problem areas are noted, informs maintenance supervisor on production log form.

   E. Maintains electronic parts inventory. Prepares electronic parts requisitions and forwards to purchasing office. Receives parts from supply and stores in electronic parts locker.

STAFFING A SMALL BUSINESS

4. **Machines, tools, equipment and work aids used:**

    test lights   hand tools (personal tools)
    ohmmeters   blueprints
    volt meters   wiring diagrams
    circuit simulators   machine specifications
    shop tools

5. **Supervision received:**

Works under maintenance team supervisor.
Works with production supervisor, as needed, in resolving problems.

6. **Supervision given:**

None

7. **Regular contacts** (Internal and external required in the job; consider frequency, type and complexity):

Internal: Team supervisor - daily.
Production supervisor - as needed and in weekly maintenance team meeting.
Maintenance workers - as needed and in weekly maintenance team meeting.
Production employees - as required in performing job.

External: none.

Part B. Requirements of the employee.

1. **Training:**

   A. General education.

   High school diploma or GED

   B. Vocational preparation (includes vocational education, apprenticeship, college training, on-the-job training).

   Military or civilian basic electronics technician course.

   Two years apprenticeship.

   Six months OJT in this company. Supervisor must certify applicant is qualified to perform electronic technician duties with limited direct supervision.

HUMAN RESOURCE RECRUITMENT PLANNING

2. Aptitudes and personal traits required of a worker in this specific job position:

   A. Adaptability to situations requiring precise attainment of set standards.

   B. Adaptability to performing work in situations where limited information is provided.

   C. Adaptability to performing a variety of duties, often changing from one task to another, without loss of efficiency or composure.

   D. Adaptability to performing under stress when confronted with emergency or unusual situations.

3. **Physical demands** (physical requirements made of the worker by the specific job-worker situation):

   Medium to heavy work strength needed; work involves lifting and carrying; some climbing, stooping, kneeling, crouching, and crawling.

4. **Environmental conditions** (physical surroundings of job-worker situations which make specific demands upon a worker's physical capacity):

   Work location is primarily within plant; noise and machinery vibrations; summer heat may cause extreme plant temperatures.

5. Licenses, certifications, registry requirements:

   Journeyman Electronics Technician License

Additional comments:

   None

Prepared by: _____A. W. Sampson, Supervisor Electronics_____

Department: __Maintenance__   Date: __12 May 1987__

STAFFING A SMALL BUSINESS

and the duties to be performed. If the job analyzer does not possess this knowledge then the data must be interpreted by one who is trained in these areas. This usually does not become a problem unless the tasks performed are highly technical in nature or unless local, state or federal statutes define who can do what, depending on one's training, certification, or licensing. If the business uses union workers, then union regulations must also be consulted.

Job Description

This statement is generally less detailed than the data contained in the job analysis. A basic job description contains six parts:

o Title of job position,

o Where the job is located in the company,

o Title of supervisor,

o Narrative description of the job,

o Description or list of tasks performed, and

o Basic entry requirements.

The job description becomes the basis for advertising, selecting and filling the position, and then evaluating the performance of the person hired to do the job.

Examples of sample job descriptions are found in Charts 4-3 and 4-4. Assistance in writing job descriptions may be found in the U.S. Government's Dictionary of Occupational Titles (Fourth Edition, 1977), which presents comprehensive job descriptions for 20,000 occupations as an aid to match job requirements with worker skills. It also lists major military job titles and descriptions to aid in relating military to civilian occupations. This publication (1371 pages) is available in most public library reference sections or may be purchased from the U.S. Government Printing Office.

When preparing the requirements portion of the job description, keep in mind that it is often desirable to place someone in the job with the minimal basic requirements. Additionally, the requirements must be related to successful performance in the position. The employer must be able to present documentation that the listed requirements are necessary to perform the tasks in the job description.

If a part of the job requirement entails being tested (such as a typing or aptitude test), the employer requiring the testing must have validation criteria on the test being used. Any selection device used must be able to discriminate between those who will perform successfully on the job and those who will not.

Chart 4-3 Sample Job Description

Position: Equipment Mechanic

Department: Equipment Repair, Jones Construction Company

Supervisor: Shop Foreman

Job Description:

Skilled journeyman who does general overhaul and repair work on heavy wheeled or track construction equipment, trucks, and automobiles. Assignments are given in the form of oral instructions or written work orders from the superintendent or shop foreman. Work is subject to review in progress and upon completion. Works in department garage; industrial environment. Travels to job locations throughout three-county work area. May work outdoors in all kinds of weather.

Tasks Performed:

1. Overhaul, repair, and service automobiles, trucks, and heavy wheeled or track construction equipment (loaders, graders, tractors); may repair or replace fuel systems, differentials, drive units, brakes, suspension systems, chassis, front and rear ends, cooling systems, and accessory power equipment.

2. Tune motors using standard testing equipment.

3. Check and balance wheels for proper wheel alignment.

4. Inspect, repair, replace and align pads, cleats and tracks of tracked vehicle.

5. Make road tests to locate defects in equipment operation and as a check on repair work before the return of equipment to active use; utilize a variety of common testing devices such as ammeters, volt meters, gauges of various types, and other equipment.

6. Work on equipment at rural job location when needed.

7. Use shop tools and help keep inventory on tools.

8. Recommend purchase of needed parts.

9. Assist in keeping shop and shop tools in order.

10. Pick up needed parts at supply houses or from other companies.

11. Perform related work as assigned.

STAFFING A SMALL BUSINESS

Requirements:

1. High school education or equivalent.

2. Training as a mechanic and in use of tools required to perform job.

3. Experience as mechanic.

4. Commercial driver's license.

5. Ability to lift heavy objects.

Chart 4-4 Sample Job Description

Position: Tax Attorney

Department: Legal Staff, Metropolitan Petroleum Co., Inc.

Supervisor: Senior Corporate Attorney

Job Description: Performs responsible legal work in all tax cases filed on behalf of or against the corporation. Advises company officials on legal tax matters. Work is discussed or reviewed in progress and upon completion. Works primarily in an office or court room. Job requires travel to court location or other areas in conduct of case work, and visits to other departments and agencies.

Tasks Performed:

1. Represent corporation in all tax cases filed on behalf of or against corporation; conduct research, prepare and file briefs, appear in court.

2. Advise company officials on legal tax matters that affect the corporation; answer questions, confer with company officials and departments, perform research, prepare opinion.

3. May draft legal instruments.

4. Examine and report on changes and revisions in tax laws; advise corporation on changes; direct that supplemental or revised documents be placed in office files.

5. Confer with lay people and attorneys on tax matters.

6. Perform related duties as requested.

Requirements:

- o Doctorate of Jurisprudence degree.
- o Licensed to practice law in state and Federal Court.
- o Two years' experience in tax law representation and litigation.

STAFFING A SMALL BUSINESS

It is not legal to require testing which has not been validated or to list job requirements not necessary to successfully do the job. More detailed information on this topic is found in the Federal "Uniform Guidelines on Employee Selection, 1978 Revision." This document was developed by the Equal Opportunity Commission, the Office of Federal Contracts Compliance, the Civil Service Commission, and the Department of Justice. (See Chapter 5.)

When the job description is finalized and legally correct, the next step is to begin the recruiting process.

Developing Recruitment Sources

Recruiting for a new position should begin within the business. Filling a position with current employees tends to reinforce the company's commitment to upward mobility and acknowledges its willingness to reward good performance and loyalty. Further, it raises employee morale and satisfaction by keeping workers informed and giving them the opportunity to move up within the company.

If an internal search fails to yield qualified candidates then external recruiting sources must be used. There are several sources to be considered.

People send blind job applications and resumes to all kinds of businesses. Many firms automatically discard any unsolicited job applications; other companies file them away until a position becomes available. They can be an excellent initial source of external job candidates. If a job application or resume matches an opening, all it takes is a phone call to determine if the person is still interested in a job.

Direct advertising (local newspapers, trade magazines, etc.) is a common method used to develop a pool of applicants. Newspapers are quick and reach a large portion of the local population. Trade magazines focus on a particular group of people but take several weeks or months before replies begin to appear. Trade magazine advertising is usually done when a business wants to reach a particular segment of people who possess special credentials crucial to the advertised position.

Employment agencies are another good source of job applicants. They can be expensive (if private) but the agency does the initial screening to ensure that the candidate is qualified. Sometimes the company seeking an employee pays the fee; at other times the applicant pays the fee. State employment agencies also do the initial screening and send qualified people to the company for interviews. State agencies tend to place more people in the lower levels of employment.

Placement offices of schools and colleges are in the business of locating positions for their graduates. Placement officers maintain files on graduates seeking employment as well as on companies seeking employees. The office serves as a liaison between graduates and companies.

HUMAN RESOURCE RECRUITMENT PLANNING

Other sources are labor unions; friends or relatives of current employees; jobbers, suppliers or sales representatives who call on your business; and temporary help agencies. Chart 4-5 is an example of how to list and compare different recruiting sources to assist in improving the company's recruiting efforts.

Knowing where to go and who to see can save time and energy in locating qualified people.

STAFFING A SMALL BUSINESS

Chart 4-5 Example of Recruiting Sources Chart

Source	Contact	Type of Applicants	Cost	Time to Reach Applicant	Previous Results
Globe-Times Newspaper	Want Ads Classified 555-2921 ext. 61	Mostly high school, some with college courses	$19 for 5 day ad 20 words maximum	Next day	Good for beginning positions. Not good for managers
Professional Management monthly trade journal	Positions available section (888) 555-3030 ext. 293	Managers. Both new graduates and experienced people	$150 per month for 3 line, 1 column ad	2 months, but journal has 40,000 subscribers	Good for high paying management positions
Acme Employment Agency	Miss Betts Counselor 555-1223	High school level. Some college	$50 to obtain candidates $100 if one is selected	Usually within 1 week	Very good selection of non-college employees
State University	Don Vern Placement Director 555-9872	College graduates. Part-time students	Free	December, June, August for graduates. Part-time always	Good source for new college graduates
Employees	Anyone	All kinds	Free	Immediate if any are available	Employees know abilities of those they recommend
Carson Wholesalers	Sam Black Sales Rep 555-3708	Sales and management	Free	Depends on what is available	Excellent. Sam knows everybody in the business

HUMAN RESOURCE RECRUITMENT PLANNING

Worksheet 4-1 Job Sheet

Department:

1. What is your job called?

2. Who is your **immediate senior** and what is his/her job called?

3. If you have **immediate juniors** what are their jobs called?

4. What tasks do you carry out? (List duties in order of importance and after each task estimate percentage of time spent on the task).

Signature   Date

STAFFING A SMALL BUSINESS

Worksheet 4-2 Job Analysis

A job analysis is an evaluation of the duties and responsibilities of a job. It details what a worker does, how, why, and the circumstances under which it is done. The information collected from this job analysis will be used to develop a job description for various job positions.

Job title: **Department:**

Employment classification:

Part A. Requirements of the job.

1. Job summary (A brief statement covering purpose and nature of the job):

2. Work performed:

3. Description of tasks:

4. Machines, tools, equipment and work aids used:

5. Supervision received:

6. Supervision given:

7. Regular contacts (internal and external required in the job; consider frequency, type and complexity):

HUMAN RESOURCE RECRUITMENT PLANNING

Part B: **Requirements of the employee.**

1. Training:

    A. General education.

    B. Vocational preparation. (Includes vocational education, apprenticeship, college training, on-the-job training.)

2. Aptitudes and personal traits required of a worker in this specific job position:

3. Physical demands (physical requirements made of the worker by the specific job-worker situation):

4. Environmental conditions (physical surroundings of job-worker situations which make specific demands upon a worker's physical capacity):

5. Licenses, certifications, registry requirements:

Additional comments:

Prepared by:

Department: Date:

4 - 17

STAFFING A SMALL BUSINESS

Worksheet 4-3 Job Description

Position:

Department:

Supervisor:

Job Description:

Tasks Performed:

Requirements:

Chapter 5
Legal Implications of Staffing

Summary of Chapter

Many federal laws establish clearcut regulations involving employment practices and employee compensation. Numerous court decisions have impressed upon the business community the necessity for managers and employers to be aware of the legislation that affects their employees or their work environment. This chapter will examine the laws and orders that can have an immediate and binding effect on employment decisions. The laws and orders are divided into three areas: employment, compensation, and health and safety.

Employment Laws and Orders

Title VII of the Civil Rights Act of 1964

Purpose: The principal federal law relating to most types of employment discrimination, its purpose is to give everyone an equal chance to obtain employment. The law has a number of objectives:

- o It outlaws certain discriminatory employment practices.

- o It created a federal agency to enforce the law and gave it regulatory powers.

- o It sets penalties for violators of the law.

- o It requires state laws to uphold Title VII.

- o It requires that certain records be maintained by designated persons or agencies.

- o It does not alter state or federal veterans' preference laws.

Title VII prohibits employment discrimination based on race, religion, sex, color, or national origin. Employers are also prohibited from discriminatory practices regarding:

- o Recruiting and hiring
- o Job advertising

STAFFING A SMALL BUSINESS

- o Ability and experience
- o Occupational qualification
- o Testing
- o Prehire inquiries
- o Employment status
- o Compensation
- o Merit, incentive, or seniority plans
- o Insurance, retirement, and welfare plans
- o Promotion and seniority
- o Dress and appearance
- o Leave of absence benefits
- o Discharge
- o Retirement
- o Union membership
- o Persons opposed to discriminatory practices or exercising their rights under Title VII

Regulatory agency: Equal Employment Opportunity Commission (EEOC).

Applies to: Private or public employers which have fifteen or more employees, private and public employment agencies, hiring halls, labor unions with fifteen or more members.

Penalties: Court decreed affirmative action programs and back pay.

Affirmative Action
(Executive Order 11246 signed by President Johnson in 1965.)

Purpose: This Presidential Executive Order mandates affirmative action within firms that provide goods or services for the federal government. Affirmative action requires these businesses to actively engage in recruiting, hiring, and promoting qualified women, minorities, veterans, and handicapped to attain an equitable distribution within the firm's workforce.

Regulatory agency: Office of Federal Contract Compliance Programs (OFCCP) or Civil Service Commission.

Applies to: Employers with Federal contracts over $50,000 per year must file a written affirmative action plan with OFCCP. Those with contracts from $10,000 to $50,000 must have an affirmative action plan but are not required to file it. Also applies to federal agencies and U.S. Postal Service.

Penalties: Cancellation of contract.

LEGAL IMPLICATIONS OF STAFFING

Age Discrimination in Employment Act (1967)

Purpose: The act promotes the employment of older persons based on ability rather than age; it prohibits arbitrary age discrimination in employment for workers from 40 to 70; it helps employers and workers resolve age-related employment problems.

Regulatory agency: Equal Employment Opportunity Commission.

Applies to: Private employers with 20 or more workers; all governments regardless of number of employees. Federal employment has no upper age limit. Applies also to employment agencies and unions with 25 or more members.

Penalties: Court decreed affirmative action programs, back pay, fines up to $10,000, and possible imprisonment.

Vocational Rehabilitation Act of 1973

Purpose: The act requires certain firms providing goods or services to the federal government to employ and promote qualified handicapped persons.

Regulatory agency: Office of Federal Contract Compliance Programs or Civil Service Commission.

Applies to: Any firm receiving federal contracts amounting to $2,500 or more a year.

Penalties: Cancellation of contract.

Compensation Laws

Most compensation benefits are based on the provision of the Old Age, Survivors, Disability and Health Insurance Program (OASDHI). More than 90 percent of the U.S. labor force is covered by these programs, which include Social Security, unemployment, Medicare, and Medicaid benefits. OASDHI also covers certain welfare services such as Aid to Families of Dependent Children (AFDC).

Workers' Compensation (each state has its own laws)

Purpose: It financially compensates workers or their dependents for work-related injuries, diseases, or death. Since the employer is responsible for any job-related damage a worker may sustain, laws have been enacted at the state level to institute insurance programs to cover employees.

Regulatory agency: A state industrial commission.

Applies to: Most employees except farm workers, home workers, and federal employees.

STAFFING A SMALL BUSINESS

Unemployment Compensation (Title IX of the Social Security Act - 1935)

Purpose: The act provides for financial assistance to workers who have been laid off through no fault of their own. Funds are raised through state unemployment compensation taxes. Each state maintains its own program. The program provides benefits only to employees whose employers are paying the tax. States may establish certain eligibility requirements such as a minimum length of time worked to be covered or having earned a minimum set wage.

Regulatory agency: The state unemployment commission.

Applies to: Any employer with one or more employees who worked some part of twenty or more weeks must pay federal or state unemployment tax. Also covered are employers paying wages of $1,500 or more in any calendar quarter. Some states may have more rigid requirements than the federal minimums.

Name: **Social Security Act (1935)**

Purpose: The act was originally created to provide a minimum income for retired workers. Amendments have increased coverage to compensate dependents of a deceased worker; totally disabled workers; hospital and medical insurance coverage to include Medicare for people over 65. Funding is through taxes collected from both employers and employees based on income earned. These taxes are authorized by the Federal Insurance Contributions Act (FICA).

Regulatory agency: Social Security Administration in the U.S. Department of Health and Human Services

Applies to: Most workers in the United States. Some civilian federal employees are covered instead by a federal retirement system.

Fair Labor Standards Act (1938)

Purpose: This federal law specifies a minimum hourly wage and standard workweek. Additionally, the law establishes overtime pay, equal pay, required records, and child labor standards.

Regulatory agency: The U.S. Department of Labor's Wage and Hour Division.

Applies to: All enterprises affecting interstate commerce. It includes laundries and dry cleaners, construction firms, hospitals, public and private schools, a retail or service establishment with annual gross sales of not less than $362,500, and any other business with annual gross sales of at least $250,000.

Penalties: Back pay, fines up to $10,000, and possible imprisonment.

LEGAL IMPLICATIONS OF STAFFING

Equal Pay Act of 1963 (An amendment to the Fair Labor Standards Act)

Purpose: The Equal Pay Act is a part of the Fair Labor Standards Act. It prohibits differential wages paid to men and women doing substantially the same work. If both sexes are doing the same work with similar skills, responsibility, working conditions, and effort, then the pay must be equal.

Regulatory agency: The U.S. Department of Labor's Wage and Hour Division.

Applies to: All businesses affecting interstate commerce, including local, state, and federal agencies.

Penalties: Back pay, fines up to $10,000, and possible imprisonment.

Name: **Employee Retirement Income Security Act (1974)**

Purpose: The act was enacted to ensure that private employee pension plans will actually provide something when the recipients retire and become eligible for the benefits. ERISA is a complex regulation requiring retirement plan managers to adhere to specific fiduciary duties; maintain records and reports; and remain within specified investment restrictions.

Regulatory agency: The Pension Benefit Guaranty Corporation, a federal agency, administers the plan termination insurance program (which ensures that employees obtain vested retirement rights if the plan fails). The Internal Revenue Service's Office of Employee Plans and Exempt Organizations handles tax implications; and the Department of Labor's Labor-Management Services Administration handles other aspects of managing ERISA. Congress has considered creating a single entity to be in charge: The Employee Benefits Administration.

Applies to: Employees with pension plans. ERISA requires companies with pension plans to subscribe to specific regulations regarding the administration of the plans, but it does not require employers to have any pension plans.

Name: **Individual Retirement Accounts (Revenue Act of 1978)**

Purpose: The original purpose of the act was to enable small employers to have employee retirement plans without the administrative burden of ERISA. The IRA allowed a business to pay $7,500 or up to 15 percent of an employee's gross salary (whichever is smaller) to a bank, savings and loan, mutual fund, or insurance company for investment for the employee. In 1981 it was expanded to allow employees to contribute an additional $2,000 to their company retirement fund or to their own IRA.

Regulatory agency: The Internal Revenue Service.

Applies to: Any employer or employee. For an individual to be eligible, he or she must have compensation included in their income during the year.

STAFFING A SMALL BUSINESS

Health and Safety

Occupation Safety and Health Act (1970)

Purpose: The act created regulations and enforcement practices to render the work environment safe and healthy for workers.

Regulatory agency: The Occupational Safety and Health Administration in the Department of Labor.

Applies to: Any firm affecting interstate commerce having one or more employees.

Penalties: Violation citations and fines up to $10,000 for each violation.

LEGAL IMPLICATIONS OF STAFFING

Chart 5-1 List of Equal Employment Opportunity Commission
(EEOC) Field Offices
(AO = Area Office, DO = District Office)

Albuquerque AO, 505 Marquette, NW, Suite 1515
    Albuquerque, NM 87101. . . . . 505/766-2061

Atlanta DO, 75 Piedmont Avenue NE, 10th Floor
    Atlanta, GA 30303 . . . . 404/221-4566

Baltimore DO, 711 West 40th St., Suite 210
    Baltimore, MD 21211 . . . . 301/962-3932

Birmingham DO, 2121 Eighth Avenue, North
    Birmingham, AL 35203 . . . . 205/254-1166

Boston AO, 150 Causeway St., Suite 1000
    Boston, MA 02114 . . . . 617/223-4535

Buffalo AO, One West Genessee St., Room 320
    Buffalo, NY 14202 . . . . 716/846-4441

Charlotte DO, 1301 East Morehead
    Charlotte, NC 28204 . . . . 704/371-6437

Chicago DO, 536 South Clark St., Room 234
    Chicago, IL 60605 . . . . 312/353-2713

Cincinnati AO, 550 Main St., Room 7019
    Cincinnati, OH 45202 . . . . 513/684-2379

Cleveland DO, 1365 Ontario St., Room 602
    Cleveland, OH 44114 . . . . 216/522-7425

Dallas DO, 1900 Pacific, 13th Floor
    Dallas, TX 75201 . . . . 214/767-4607

Dayton AO, 200 West Second St., Room 608
    Dayton, OH 45402 . . . . 513/225-2753

Denver DO, 1513 Stout St., 6th Floor
    Denver, CO 80202 . . . . 303/837-2771

Detroit DO, 660 Woodward Avenue, Suite 600
    Detroit, MI 48226 . . . . 313/226-7636

El Paso AO, 2211 East Missouri, Room E-235
    El Paso, TX 79903 . . . . 915/543-7596

Fresno AO, 1313 P St., Suite 103
    Fresno, CA 93721 . . . . 209/487-5793

Greensboro AO, 324 West Market St., Room 132
    Greensboro, NC 27402 . . . . 919/378-5174

STAFFING A SMALL BUSINESS

Greenville AO, 7 North Laurens St., Suite 507
    Greenville, SC 29602 . . . . 803/233-1791

Houston DO, 2320 LaBranch, Room 1101
    Houston, TX 77004 . . . . 713/226-5561

Indianapolis DO, 46 East Ohio St., Room 456
    Indianapolis, IN 46204 . . . . 317/269-7212

Jackson AO, 100 West Capitol St., Suite 721
    Jackson, MS 39201 . . . . 601/960-4537

Kansas City AO, 1150 Grand, 1st Floor
    Kansas City, MO 64106 . . . . 816/374-5773

Little Rock AO, 700 West Capitol
    Little Rock, AR 72201 . . . . 501/378-5901

Los Angeles DO, 3255 Wilshire Blvd., 9th Floor
    Los Angeles, CA 90010 . . . . 213/688-3400

Louisville AO, 600 Jefferson St.
    Louisville, KY 40202 . . . . 502/582-6082

Memphis DO, 1407 Union Ave., Suite 502
    Memphis, TN 38104 . . . . 901/521-2617

Miami DO, 300 Biscayne Blvd. Way, Suite 414
    Miami, FL 33131 . . . . 305/350-4491

Milwaukee DO, 342 North Water St., Room 612
    Milwaukee, WI 53202 . . . . 414/291-1111

Minneapolis AO, 12 South Sixth St.
    Minneapolis, MN 55402 . . . . 612/725-6101

Nashville AO, 404 James Robertson Pky., Suite 1822
    Nashville, TN 37219 . . . . 615/251-5820

Newark AO, 744 Broad St., Room 502
    Newark, NJ 07102 . . . . 201/645-6383

New Orleans DO, 600 South St.
    New Orleans, LA 70130 . . . . 504/589-3842

New York DO, 90 Church St., Room 1301
    New York, NY 10007 . . . . 212/264-7161

Norfolk AO, 200 Granby Mall, Room 412
    Norfolk, VA 23510 . . . . 804/441-3470

Oakland AO, 1515 Clay St., Room 640
    Oakland, CA 94612 . . . . 415/273-7588

Oklahoma City AO, 50 Penn Pl., Suite 1430
    Oklahoma City, OK 73118 . . . . 405/231-4912

LEGAL IMPLICATIONS OF STAFFING

Philadelphia DO, 127 North Fourth St., Suite 200
        Philadelphia, PA 19106 . . . . 215/597-7784

Phoenix DO, 201 North Central Ave., Suite 1450
        Phoenix, AZ 85073 . . . . 602/261-3882

Pittsburgh AO, 1000 Liberty Ave., Room 2038A
        Pittsburgh, PA 15222 . . . . 412/644-3444

Raleigh AO, 414 Fayetteville St.
        Raleigh, NC 27608 . . . . 919/755-4064

Richmond AO, 400 North Eighth St., Room 6213
        Richmond, VA 23240 . . . . 804/771-2692

San Antonio AO, 727 East Durango, Suite B-601
        San Antonio, TX 78206 . . . . 512/229-6051

San Diego DO, 880 Front St.
        San Diego, CA 92188 . . . . 714/293-6288

San Francisco DO, 1390 Market St., Suite 325
        San Francisco, CA 94102 . . . . 415/556-0260

San Jose AO, 84 West Santa Clara Ave. Room 300
        San Jose, CA 95113 . . . . 408/275-7352

Seattle DO, 710 Second Ave., 7th Floor
        Seattle, WA 98104 . . . . 206/442-0968

St. Louis DO, 625 North Euclid St.
        St. Louis, MO 63108 . . . . 314/425-5571

Tampa AO, 700 Twiggs St., Room 302
        Tampa, FL 33602 . . . . 813/228-2310

Washington AO, 1717 H St., NW, Suite 402
        Washington, DC 20006 . . . . 202/653-6197

STAFFING A SMALL BUSINESS

Chart 5-2 State and Municipal Offices Authorized to Administer EEOC Anti-Discrimination Programs

Alaska Commission for Human Rights
Alexandria (VA) Human Rights Office
Allentown (PA) Human Relations Commission
Anchorage (AK) Equal Right Commission
Arizona Civil Rights Division
Augusta/Richmond County (GA) Human Relations Commission
Austin (TX) Human Relations Commission

Baltimore (MD) Community Relations Commission
Bloomington (IN) Human Rights Commission
Broward County (FL) Human Relations Division

California Fair Employment Practices Commission
Charleston (WV) Human Rights Commission
Clearwater (FL) Office of Community Relations
Colorado Civil Rights Commission
Colorado State Personnel Board
Connecticut Commission of Human Rights and Opportunity
Corpus Christi (TX) Human Relations Commission

Dade County (FL) Fair Housing and Employment Commission
Delaware Department of Labor
District of Columbia Office of Human Rights

East Chicago (IN) Human Relations Commission
Evansville (IN) Human Relations Commission

Fairfax County (VA) Human Rights Commission
Florida Commission on Human Rights
Fort Wayne (IN) Metropolitan Human Relations Commission
Fort Worth (TX) Human Relations Commission

Gary (IN) Human Relations Commission
Georgia Office of Fair Employment Practices

Howard County (MD) Human Rights Commission
Hawaii Department of Labor and Industrial Relations

Idaho Commission on Human Rights
Illinois Fair Employment Practices Commission
Indiana Civil Rights Commission
Iowa Commission on Civil Rights

Jacksonville (FL) Community Relations Commission

Kansas Commission on Human Rights
Kentucky Commission on Human Rights

LEGAL IMPLICATIONS OF STAFFING

Lexington-Fayette (KY) Urban County Human Rights Commission
Lincoln (NE) Commission on Human Rights

Madison (WI) Equal Opportunities Commission
Maine Human Rights Commission
Maryland Commission on Human Relations
Massachusetts Commission Against Discrimination
Michigan Civil Rights Commission
Minneapolis (MN) Department of Civil Rights
Minnesota Department of Human Rights
Missouri Commission on Human Rights
Montana Commission on Human Rights
Montgomery County (MD) Human Relations Commission

Nebraska Equal Opportunity Commission
Nevada Commission on Equal Rights of Citizens
New Hampshire Commission for Human Rights
New Jersey Division on Civil Rights, Department of Law and Public Safety
New Mexico Human Rights Commission
New York City (NY) Commission on Human Rights
New York State Division on Human Rights
North Dakota Department of Labor

Ohio Civil Rights Commission
Oklahoma Human Rights Commission
Omaha (NE) Human Relations Department
Oregon Bureau of Labor
Orlando (FL) Human Relations Department

Pennsylvania Human Relations Commission
Philadelphia (PA) Commission on Human Relations
Prince George's County (MD) Human Relations Commission
Puerto Rico Department of Labor

Rhode Island Commission for Human Rights
Rockville (MD) Human Rights Commission

St. Louis (MO) Civil Rights Enforcement Agency
St. Paul (MN) Department of Human Rights
St. Petersburg (FL) Office of Human Rights
Seattle (WA) Human Rights Commission
Sioux Falls (SD) Human Relations Commission
South Bend (IN) Human Rights Commission
South Carolina Human Affairs Commission
South Dakota Division of Human Rights
Springfield (OH) Human Relations Department

Tacoma (WA) Human Rights Commission
Tennessee Commission for Human Development

Utah Industrial Commission

STAFFING A SMALL BUSINESS

Vermont Attorney General's Office, Civil Rights Division
Virgin Islands Department of Labor

Washington (state) Human Rights Commission
West Virginia Human Rights Commission
Wheeling (WV) Human Rights Commission
Wichita (KS) Commission Civil Rights
Wisconsin Equal Rights Division, Department of Industry,
    Labor and Human Relations
Wisconsin State Personnel Commission
Wyoming Fair Employment Practices Commission

Chapter 6
Compensation Considerations

Summary of Chapter

Compensation, direct and indirect, is one of the most powerful inducements for attracting and keeping good employees. To be successful, the total compensation package must include both financial and non-financial remuneration for services rendered. This chapter will cover the basic concepts of compensation and examine different combinations that can be used to meet the needs of the organization and its employees.

Compensation Factors

The primary purpose of compensation—to reward workers for services rendered—is simple, yet developing adequate compensation can be a frustrating, complex exercise. Compensation policy is affected by several factors:

o   The size and qualifications of the labor pool. If needed workers are in short (or ample) supply, the cost to acquire them can be high (or low). The availability of training resources and support for technological advances affect the size and qualifications of the labor pool.

o   The financial strength of the business (productivity). A prosperous business can afford to spend money to reward employees and to obtain quality people. A weak company may not be able to offer a strong compensation package.

o   Inflation and the cost of living. Inflation can turn a highly competitive compensation plan into a less than adequate program in a few short years.

o   Unions. Whether a part of your business or not, unions can affect company compensation practices. Most publicized union-management debates appear to center on compensation.

o   Government. Local, state and federal entities dictate much of what has to be considered in developing a total compensation package.

Recognizing the influence of these factors, a total compensation program should serve these purposes:

o   Attract quality people to run the business.

STAFFING A SMALL BUSINESS

o   Motivate and retain those employees who, by their increased productivity, increase the value of the business.

o   Create a rewarding and satisfying environment which is conducive to furthering the goals and strategies of the business.

Compensation planning begins with a concept of the worth of the position. Just as a job description is based on the tasks to be performed, not the qualities of any specific individual, the worth of a position is considered first, not the worth of the person who fills it.

Determining Worth of a Job

The job description is the basis for determining the worth of a job. The central concept of any compensation program is that of determining a basic monetary value for the performance of a specific job.

Determining what is an equitable and fair value for a position is done by developing a wage and salary survey. Begin with your business as outlined in Chart 6-1. Using business connections, local knowledge of the area, and the Yellow Pages, select similar businesses and inquire about their compensation practices. In many areas this research is being done on an annual basis by a local chamber of commerce or business school. Sometimes the information is free, other times there may be a fee.

How many businesses should one survey? In a community of 150,000 or fewer people, six to ten businesses should suffice. As a rule of thumb, when the responses over six do not change the findings, then you have enough data. As the market area increases (regional or statewide), then more positions should be surveyed, with twenty to thirty firms being a reasonable number to contact. Nationwide surveys may include up to 2000 different firms.

When the data have been collected, compare the businesses, their markets, and their different types of compensation. Personal knowledge of the firms, products, and people can also help in understanding how their compensation relates to the quality of the employees.

The results of this survey become the keystone for developing a basic wage structure. To help understand how compensation increases with experience and longevity, survey several similar positions in each company. For example, several levels of carpenter positions in the construction companies surveyed might be listed (see Chart 6-2) to determine various entry, mid- and upper-level salaries.

COMPENSATION CONSIDERATIONS

Chart 6-1 Wage and Salary Survey, Single Job Level

	Your Business	Comparison Businesses		
Name of Business	Ajax Construction	Acme Builders	Wendel's Home Construction Company	Greeley Development Corporation
Address	1020 Sand Rd. Anytown	20 Industry Rd. Anytown	Old County Rd. Anytown	City Limits Rd. Anytown
Industry	Home Construction	Home Construction	Home Construction	Residential Development
Principal Market Served	Within 50 miles of Anytown	Within 50 miles of Anytown	Primarily Anytown area	Northwest region of state
Size of Market or Business Output	3 - 8 houses at a time	5 - 10 houses at a time	6 - 8 houses at a time	10 - 20 houses at a time
Number of Employees (Including management)	15	19	18	38
Positions Surveyed	Journeyman Carpenter	Journeyman Carpenter	Journeyman	Framer
Normal Work Week	40 hours	40 hours	40 hours	40 hours
Unionized	No	No	No	No
Basic Wage/Salary	?	$7.95/hr	$8.50/hr	$9.10/hr
Other Benefits	?	SS, WC, health, OT	SS, WC, health	SS, WC health
Vacations/ Holidays	?	None	None	One week, no paid holidays
Remarks:		Low turnover. Usually 10 hrs per week OT. Keep crews on through winter	Good quality work. Tends to cut back in winter.	Company has high standards. Drive men hard. High turnover

SS = Social Security   WC - Workers' Compensation   OT = Overtime
Basic Wage Range: $7.95 - $9.10   Average: $8.52

6 - 3

Establishing a Basic Wage Structure

The wage and salary survey data provide benchmarks for further analysis. When fitting new positions into an ongoing organization, the compensation must correspond to the existing organizational structure. Three primary factors are considered when developing the wage structure for the new position(s):

1. The range of compensation being paid in similar positions, as determined from the survey.

2. The worth or value of the new position to the company, based on degrees of
    o skills required,
    o responsibility assumed,
    o effort required, and
    o working conditions.

3. The present compensation ranges in the company.

Newly created positions may or may not fit into an existing job grouping in the business. Here is an example.

Assume that a retail sales outlet for a home appliance product has expanded to create a new service department. This new department calls for a manager, three service people, and a combination secretary-receptionist-billing clerk. The manager and service people must all be trained repair people, skills not previously required in the business. This forms a new job grouping. These four positions might represent two to four levels in the category of repair people. One might be an entry level or apprentice position, one or more might be for experienced repair people. One position might be a repair supervisor, and the managerial position would involve the product technical skills as well as the administrative-managerial skills. These four positions have become a career progression program as well as a job classification (see Chart 6-3).

The other position, secretary-receptionist-billing clerk, might fit into a job grouping already in the business. The only difference between this position and a similar one in sales might be the technical product language used: in sales the person would deal with billing for the product line, whereas in service the person would bill for parts and repairs. Other job functions would be similar.

At this point it might be helpful to review and understand terms used in creating a wage and salary structure.

   o Job classification. The levels consisting of degree of training, experience, or longevity which are found within a particular job or position. They are also referred to as job grades.

6 - 4

COMPENSATION CONSIDERATIONS

Chart 6-2 Wage and Salary Survey, Multiple Job Levels

	Your Business	Comparison Businesses		
Name of Business	Ajax Construction	Acme Builders	Wendel's Home Construction Company	Greeley Development Corporation
Position	Carpenter's helper	Carpenter's helper	Carpenter's trainee	Framer apprentice
Experience	Apprentice	None	None	None
Basic Wage/Salary	?	$4.75/hr	$4.20/hr	$4.85/hr
Other Benefits	?	SS, WC, health, OT	SS, WC, health	SS, WC health
Vacations/Holidays	?	None	None	None
Position	Journeyman carpenter	Journeyman carpenter	Journeyman carpenter	Framer
Experience	One year	18 months	One year	1 to 1.5 yr
Basic Wage/Salary	?	$7.95/hr	$8.50/hr	$9.10/hr
Other Benefits	?	SS, WC, health, OT	SS, WC, health	SS, WC health
Vacations/Holidays	?	None	None	One week, no paid holidays
Position	Carpenter supervisor	Carpenter crew chief	Carpenter supervisor	Framer crew foreman
Experience	5-10 years	8-12 years	5-9 years	4-6 years
Basic Wage/Salary	?	$12.00/hr	$12.50/hr	$13.00/hr
Other Benefits	?	SS, WC, health, OT	SS, WC, health	SS, WC health
Vacations/Holidays	?	One week no holidays	One week no holidays	Two weeks, no paid holidays
Range of all Positions	$ -$	$4.75-$12.00	$4.70-$12.50	$4.85-$13.00

STAFFING A SMALL BUSINESS

o Job grouping. Jobs which are individually different but because of a similarity of job functions can be grouped into categories such as sales, repair, administration, or secretarial.

o Wage/salary range. The spread of wages or salary paid, from the entry level position to the highest pay that could be earned, is the wage/salary range. Alternatively, the range is the spread found within a particular classification or grade. This range is based on length of service while the first range is based on promotions.

A typical wage/salary table lists rows and columns of salaries. Each row represents a different job classification (job grade). Each column represents a specific pay level, called a step, within each grade. Each complete row represents the lowest to the highest salary within each job classification (grade). Chart 6-4 is called a five-by-five compensation or salary table. Each progression across in rows or down in columns represents a five percent increase in salary. The changes can be any percentage desired.

Grade changes come about only through promotion to another classification. Step increases can be based on longevity, merit, or both. A recommendation for the five-by-five salary schedule might be as follows:

Step 1   Basic entry salary for each grade (job classification). This step applies for the first year of employment.

Step 2   Pay raise upon successful completion of one year in Step 1 and approval of supervisor.

Step 3   Pay raise upon successful completion of one year in Step 2 and approval of supervisor.

Step 4   Merit raise I

Step 5   Merit raise II

Step 6   Merit raise III

Increases to the last three steps (4, 5, and 6) are based on merit, not length of employment. The personnel are selected according to the company merit system.

A salary schedule using this percentage format can easily be established by starting grade 1, step 1 at the current lowest paid salary in the company. If there is a chance that some new positions might begin at a lower rate than presently paid, start your current lowest salary at grade 2 or 3, step 1 and then work backward by whatever percentage is selected. The sample salary schedule (Chart 6-4) is based on a monthly salary, but it could just as easily be weekly or hourly, whichever way the company pays its employees.

Setting up a salary schedule is not really difficult. Assigning individual job positions to specific grades is not as easy.

COMPENSATION CONSIDERATIONS

Chart 6-3 Career Progression Pattern
(Job Classification Chart)

Job Title	Duties	Experience Required
Apprentice Repair Person	Assist repair person to disassemble, diagnose, repair and assemble appliance products. Works under supervision.	1. Basic training or schooling in small appliance repair procedures.
Journeyman Repair Person	Disassemble, diagnose, repair and assemble appliance products. Supervise apprentice.	1. Basic training or schooling in small appliance repair procedures. 2. Advanced training in appliance products repair. 3. Minimum one year apprenticeship experience.
Repair Supervisor	Disassemble, diagnose, repair and assemble products. Knowledge of parts ordering and billing procedures. Supervise all repair people.	1. Basic training or schooling in small appliance repair procedures. 2. Advanced training in appliance products repair. 3. Knowledge of product parts ordering and billing procedures. 4. Minimum one year journeyman repair experience.
Service Manager	Overall responsibility for operation of repair department.	1. All requirements for repair supervisor. 2. College level training or OJT experience in management. 3. Minimum one year repair supervisor experience.

STAFFING A SMALL BUSINESS

Determining Individual Wage Rates

Based on the data accumulated in the wage and salary survey, a salary range (grade) can be selected. If the position is to be filled with someone at the bottom end of the salary range (i.e., inexperienced), then select a grade for which there is room for increases within the salary range determined in the survey.

Referring back to Chart 6-2, the range for carpenters is from $4.70 per hour for a carpenter trainee to $13.00 per hour for a frame crew foreman. Calculate an average for each position: $4.75 for the apprentice, $8.52 for the journeyman, and $12.50 for the supervisor. This could represent a mid-point within each grade (either step 3 or 4 in a series of six).

Convert the hourly pay to a monthly pay (hourly wage times 8 hours per day times 22 work days per month) and it looks like this:

- apprentice: $836.00
- journeyman: $1500.00
- supervisor: $2200.00

Using the salary schedule (Chart 6-4 it is easy to see that the apprentice position could begin at grade 1, step 1. The salary does not allow any flexibility because it is at the bottom of this salary schedule.

For the journeyman salary of $1500 there are any number of points where it could fit; anywhere from grade 8, step 6 to grade 13, step 1. Since the $1500 is an average calculation it might be best to locate it in a grade 10, step 4 position; or grade 11, step 3 position. If a journeyman carpenter should not be that high gradewise, then a grade 9 would still accommodate the position but the $1500 average salary now becomes the high side of the range (within grade 9 the range is $1229 to $1568, which translates to an hourly wage of $6.98 to $8.91).

When assigning individual wage or salary ranges, it is best to start with the average or mid-point salary and then work out to the high and low extremes (the highest you would ever pay for that position to the lowest you could pay and still be able to hire a qualified worker). This method just makes it easier to establish realistic and usable salary ranges for each position.

Establishing the salary range for a position is only part of the total compensation plan. The other benefits comprise the rest of the program.

Other Compensation Considerations

In addition to the wage or salary paid to workers there can be a variety of other benefits. Chart 6-5 lists the most common benefits found in many company compensation plans. It also lists other benefits which are not as common with small businesses but are legitimate compensation additions.

COMPENSATION CONSIDERATIONS

Chart 6-4 Sample Salary Schedule (Paid Monthly)

Five Percent Between Grades
Five Percent Between Steps

	Steps					
Grades	1	2	3	4	5	6
1	$831	$873	$917	$963	$1011	$1062
2	873	917	963	1011	1062	1115
3	917	963	1011	1062	1115	1171
4	963	1011	1062	1115	1171	1229
5	1011	1062	1115	1171	1229	1298
6	1062	1115	1171	1229	1298	1355
7	1115	1171	1229	1298	1355	1422
8	1171	1229	1298	1355	1422	1493
9	1229	1298	1355	1422	1493	1568
10	1298	1355	1422	1493	1568	1646
11	1355	1422	1493	1568	1646	1729
12	1422	1493	1568	1646	1729	1816
13	1493	1568	1646	1729	1816	1906
14	1568	1646	1729	1816	1906	2001
15	1646	1729	1816	1906	2001	2101

Each step represents a pay increase awarded on longevity or merit. It is an increase within a specific job position. Step increases represent a change in pay without a change in job status.

Each grade represents a pay difference as assigned to a specific job (e.g., clerk typist, executive secretary, repair supervisor, service department manager). A grade increase represents a promotion from one job classification (grade) to another.

STAFFING A SMALL BUSINESS

A company can have a very basic benefit program offering a one-week paid vacation, some form of a participating pension program, and a basic form of medical insurance coverage. The company may serve only as an administrator of these programs, with all costs being deducted from the employee's salary, to a sharing of the costs by both the employee and the company, to the company paying all benefit costs.

Some companies provide a certain amount of money each month for each employee to apply as he or she sees fit to a "menu" of different benefits. This is attractive to workers in two-income families; it allows a husband and wife to select benefits from each employer that maximize rather than duplicating their coverages.

Extra benefits cost a business money. Recent compensation surveys reveal that company benefit programs can cost as much as 25 to 30 percent more than the basic wage or salary paid. Like all business expenses, benefits become another part of the cost of doing business. A good company compensation program is a strategic concept for:

o   Attracting good employees

o   Retaining good employees

o   Motivating productivity

o   Reinforcing positive employee-employer relations

o   Projecting a good public image

When deciding what other benefits should make up a compensation package, certain factors need to be carefully weighed and considered.

Cost. The expenditures must generate a return, such as increasing the ability to attract and maintain a qualified workforce. Otherwise the company cannot afford the compensation program, and what is designed to improve productivity becomes a liability.

Being Beneficial. Additional benefits must actually meet a need. A reserved parking slot one-quarter mile away from the office probably is of questionable value. Benefits should be attractive to as many employees as possible. Good benefit programs are basic in meeting needs (medical, accidental disability and death coverage, and retirement benefits) yet broad enough to be easily handled administratively.

Educating the Employee. An effective compensation program successfully communicates to employees exactly what they have as added benefits for working for the company. Pointing out the benefits in detail is an important part of the recruiting process. As long as the company provides benefits, employees should know what they are and what they cost the company. An educated employee is better able to recognize the full impact of the compensation program.

COMPENSATION CONSIDERATIONS

Chart 6-5 Compensation Benefits

Typical Benefits

Shift differentials
Overtime
Holiday pay
Separation pay
Group insurance plans
Education programs
Retirement plans
Stock options
Social Security
Workers' Compensation
Rest breaks
Vacations
Sick leave
Service recognition
Company automobiles
Bonus plan
Profit sharing
Uniforms and/or uniform cleaning service
Company products or services at a reduced cost

Other Benefits

Company paid services (legal, moving, medical, financial)
Personal loans
Recreational facilities
Club memberships
Paid vacation trips
Discount purchase privileges
Free entertainment tickets (sports, theater, opera)
Reserved parking places
Home mortgage assistance
Home selling assistance
Housing allowances (or housing provided)
Dependents' education assistance

STAFFING A SMALL BUSINESS

Putting It All Together

The options available for designing a total compensation program are infinite. Three considerations should be kept in mind: cost to the company; meeting the needs of the employees; and ease of administration.

Some components of a compensation program are regulated by federal or state statutes. Social Security, ERISA, Workers' Compensation, unemployment insurance, tax deductions, and the record-keeping requirements are outlined by law. These must be followed as regulated.

A company should look at what similar businesses are offering and also what trends are apparent in the local labor pool market areas.

Keeping up with inflation or cost-of-living increases should be considered each year. This can be an easy matter to deal with. If the annual cost of living increases four percent, just increase all figures in the salary schedule by four percent.

While the compensation program is viewed by the business as the total cost to the company, the workers see it as what their net income is after all deductions. Good administration ensures that all employees realize how much the company is contributing for their benefit, not only each payday, but for what they will also receive in the future.

Chart 6-6 is an example of a benefit program and what it costs both the company and the employee. Note that the administrative costs for setting up and maintaining benefit programs are not included in these costs.

Places to obtain information on the benefits provided and costs for additional compensation programs include:

o   Local insurance companies,

o   Unions,

o   Professional organizations in the industry,

o   Similar businesses, and

o   State agencies such as the controller's office.

COMPENSATION CONSIDERATIONS

Chart 6-6 Typical Deductions to Support a Compensation Plan

Position ____Motel Manager_____

Gross Monthly Salary ____$2485.50_____

Employer		Employee	
Salary Paid	$2485.50	Gross Income	$2485.50
Plus		Deductions	
Social Security (FICA 7.15%)	177.71	Federal withholding tax	497.10
Retirement contribution 7%	165.29	Retirement (7% of pay)	165.29
Insurance program	80.00	Social Security (FICA 7.15%)	177.71
1/12 of paid vacations		State withholding tax	140.50
and holidays (22 days)	207.13	Net Pay	$1504.90
Total cost to company	$3115.63	Deductions for this employee cost $980.60 or 39.5% of gross earnings.	

Total benefits (above cost of salary) cost this employer $630.13 or 25% above the salary.

Note: Administrative costs to the company are not included.

6 - 13

STAFFING A SMALL BUSINESS

Worksheet 6-1 Compensation Plan Costs to Company

Position

Monthly wage or salary

Employer		Employee	
Base Gross Salary	$ _____	Base Gross Salary	$ _____
Additions		Deductions	
Social Security (FICA)	_____	Federal withholding tax	_____
Workers' Compensation	_____	State withholding tax	_____
Unemployment	_____	Social Security (FICA)	_____
Retirement	_____	Retirement	_____
Insurance	_____	Insurance	_____
Paid holidays	_____	Savings program	_____
Paid vacations	_____	Stock options	_____
Profit sharing	_____	Other _____	_____
Other _____	_____		_____
Total Additions	$ _____	Total Deductions	$ _____
Salary + Additions	$ _____	Net Salary	$ _____

$$\frac{\text{Total Additions}}{\text{Gross Salary}} = \text{Percentage of Employer Contribution Above Salary}$$

$$\frac{}{} = \underline{} \%$$

$$\frac{\text{Total Deductions}}{\text{Gross Salary}} = \text{Percentage of Employee Contributions}$$

$$\frac{}{} = \underline{} \%$$

NOTE: This cost does not include administrative costs.

FICA Rate Schedule for Employers and Employees

Years	Retirement, Survivors & Disability Insurance		Hospital Insurance		Total
1986-89	5.7%	+	1.45%	=	7.15%
1990	6.2%	+	1.45%	=	7.65%

Chapter 7
Unions

Summary of Chapter

This chapter presents information on the legal aspects of unionism and the procedures involved in forming a union, collective bargaining, grievance procedures, labor disputes, and management's relations with unions.

While many businesses may never have to deal directly with unions, union activities, agreements, legislation, and even publicity affect the workplace nationwide. Many business practices and compensation benefits which are considered customary today are the results of past union efforts.

A familiarity with the terms and procedures associated with unions gives the owner/manager a broader perspective for understanding and evaluating union activities. This knowledge should enable the owner/manager to better develop strategies relative to union activities, whether the business is unionized or not.

Understanding Unions

Researchers have found that employees who are dissatisfied with some aspect of their employment conditions view union representation as a possible means for improvement. Unionism is not always seen as an alternative for dealing with management, but the primary purpose of unions is to form a cohesive block for negotiating with management.

Unions are non-profit, private organizations whose main focus is to advance the employment interests of their members. Businesses that are unionized must work with the local branch of a union, which in most cases is part of a national organization representing a particular industry or craft. Union strength is demonstrated in its power of collective bargaining: a process of negotiating and committing to writing agreements between the union and a specific business entity regarding employment conditions.

National Labor Relations Act

The National Labor Relations Act (Wagner Act) of 1935 had two functions:
- o   It provided a means for employees to stipulate if they desired a union, and
- o   It established a code of unfair labor practices which applied to employers, not employees.

The Taft-Hartley Act (or the Labor-Management Relation Act) of 1947 provided a new code of unfair labor practices binding on both management and labor. The Landrum-Griffin Act of 1959 regulated the internal activities of a union and prohibited management from making payments to a union to influence negotiations.

The National Labor Relations Act created the National Labor Relations Board (NLRB), the forum for trying unfair labor practices defined by the act. The NLRB functions as both a court and an administrative agency. Complaints are initiated by management or labor (union).

Not all employees are governed by the National Labor Relations Act. For example, municipal, state and federal employees are exempt, as are managers, supervisors, independent contractors, domestic employees, agricultural workers, employees working for spouses or parents, and employees covered by the Railway Labor Act.

Those businesses the NLRB does cover include:

o Retailers with annual sales of $500,000 or more

o Wholesalers having an annual interstate outflow and inflow of $50,000 or more

o Local transportation systems with gross revenues of $250,000 or more

o Firms operating office buildings with annual gross revenues of $100,000 or more

o Interstate transportation businesses

o Newspapers having annual gross revenues of $250,000 or more and having some interstate contacts

o Communication businesses with annual gross revenues of $100,000 or more

o Lodging businesses with annual gross revenues of $500,000 or more

o All privately operated health care institutions

When an unfair labor practice complaint is filed with the NLRB local office, the complaint is investigated. If the investigation finds a violation did occur, then a NLRB judge will hear the case and render a decision. The NLRB also oversees the process of forming a union.

Forming a Union

Union organization procedures receive considerable protection under current laws. To begin with, some group must acknowledge a need for workers to be unionized. It could be the workers or it could be a union.

Next, union representatives must collect signatures on authorization cards signifying that union representation is desired. If 30 percent of the employees sign the cards, the union can continue the organization process.

During this process neither management nor the union organizers may resort to violence, threats or coercion to attempt to sway the employees. Discipline or discharge of employees engaged in unionizing activities is prohibited.

Union organizers may present why they see the union as an advantage to employees and what the union can do to improve current employment conditions. Management also has the right to point out disadvantages such as the cost of belonging to a union versus the benefits, or how collective bargaining may not be advantageous on an individual basis.

The National Labor Relations Board becomes involved by receiving a petition for election from a union that has enough authorization cards. If the NLRB determines that sufficient interest in having a union does exist, it then must define the bargaining unit, that is, the group of employees that the union would represent.

After the bargaining unit has been selected, both the union and management can begin the pre-election campaigning. Each side must adhere to strict legal guidelines as to what can or cannot be done.

The election is supervised by the NLRB and is by secret ballot. The union is in if 50 percent plus one vote are in favor of unionizing. If the vote goes against the union, it cannot hold another election for a year. The NLRB will certify the union if it wins. The NLRB conducts approximately 3,500 elections each year; 43 to 48 percent of the elections favor the unions. Once a union is certified, the employer is required to bargain with that union on behalf of those employees it represents.

Decertification of a union by NLRB election can also occur if 30 percent of the employees request it. The majority of the employees must vote the union out.

Collective Bargaining

The NLRB requires employers to bargain with unions for wages, hours and other conditions of employment including the grievance process. Collective bargaining is both the process between union representatives and management to arrive at a written contract that is acceptable to both groups and the process by which the contract is administered and enforced.

Collective bargaining ideally should take place in a cooperative atmosphere. Collective bargaining strategies for the small business are not necessarily similar to that of larger organizations. In many cases the areas of negotiation between the management of a small business and a union will have been unofficially established by the collective bargaining of the same union and a much larger business. Also, federal and state laws will have an impact on the negotiating process by mandating minimum wages, maximum hours, safety requirements, and working conditions.

Successful collective bargaining depends to a great extent on the past relations management has maintained with its labor force. The more labor perceives management as honestly concerned with the workers' welfare and compensation, and vice versa, the easier the bargaining process.

Both sides should first do research to better understand the ramifications of the demands and counter demands. Law requires all bargaining to be conducted in good faith; there are penalties if one side or the other uses tactics detrimental to this process.

Each side usually develops a bargaining position in which there is a general settlement range that if agreed upon by the other side would be acceptable. Additionally, each side has an upper (or lower) limit in which yielding would not be acceptable. Thus, negotiating begins with each side presenting the initial demands.

As an example, a union might be negotiating for a $2.00 an hour raise. Management might see $1.00 an hour as acceptable. The union might open at $2.50 per hour and management may counter with an offer of 50 cents an hour. Through the negotiating process they might settle on a $1.50 per hour raise.

The worst outcome of not being able to reach agreement can be the union's refusal to continue to work (a strike) or management's refusal to allow workers to continue to work (a lockout). Lockouts are seldom used as a negotiating tool, and strikes usually depend as much on the economic health of the industry and the location as on the disparity of agreement conditions.

Labor Disputes and Grievance Procedures

A labor dispute occurs when one side or the other believes that the provisions of the contract have been violated. A grievance occurs when a union employee believes that his or her rights under the contract have been violated.

The grievance process begins by contacting the supervisor and attempting to resolve it at that level. If that is unsuccessful, the employee meets with the management representative to seek redress. If that fails, the union representatives meet with management to work out the problem. If that fails, then the disagreement is submitted to a binding arbitrator.

An arbitrator is a labor law expert, a neutral party, who is paid by both the union and management to hear both sides and arrive at a decision usually binding on both parties. Depending on the cost of the issue at stake, it is usually best to arrive at a decision before seeking arbitration as it typically costs each side over $700 to hire an arbitrator.

Management Relations with Unions

Being unionized is often seen by management as disadvantageous. Freedom to deal with employees can be limited, and having to deal with elected representatives, rather than individuals, can be frustrating.

An organization whose management philosophy and practice is to treat employees in the best possible way all the time, probably will not have to be concerned with unionization. Employees who have input on working hours, benefits, wages, working conditions, promotions, discipline, and other areas affecting their jobs generally do not view union membership as needed. A company should ensure that it has a means to hear complaints and a fair system to address grievances.

These same concepts apply even if workers are unionized; the main difference is that many of these conditions will be required by written contract.

Some of the ways to curtail grievances in a unionized business is for management to:

o   Make sure that all rules of conduct are communicated to all employees.

o   Have a fair and impartial system to hear grievances and investigate them.

o   Involve the union in the complaint.

o   Consider all aspects of the complaint and the worker's record since being employed.

o   Ensure that all supervisory and management personnel are thoroughly familiar with the grievance process and the company philosophy toward its employees.

A unionized company, by the fact of being unionized, requires much more attention to union contract provisions and employee rights. Good managers and employers see to it that all of the company's managers and supervisors are thoroughly educated in the provisions of the contract and labor relations procedures.

Chapter 8

Recruiting

Summary of Chapter

The previous chapters have discussed how to determine what is needed to fill a position, what laws affect filling that position, financial considerations for compensation, and development of recruiting sources. This chapter concentrates primarily on methods used to create a pool of qualified applicants and the application form itself. This chapter will clearly explain what can and cannot legally be asked on an application form.

Advertising

The recruiting sources considered in Chapter 4 cover two primary methods of developing a job applicant pool: (1) the company advertises the position and then conducts the initial screening process itself, and (2) an outside agency recruits and screens the applicants. Either method uses a procedure to limit the applicants to those who have specific qualifications. The screening process should begin with the advertisement. Consider this newspaper ad, for example:

> Wanted: high school graduate with experience in retail sales to serve as company representative for established national brand shoe manufacturer. Work involves extensive travel, own automobile needed. Pay and benefits competitive. Contact 555-555-1223, ext. 73. Ask for Miss Bell.

The ad clearly establishes four conditions that restrict the potential applicants: (1) high school graduate, (2) retail sales experience, (3) willingness and ability to travel, and (4) access to a vehicle.

Even if an employer announces a vacancy informally to an employee, conditions are set, usually implicitly:

> "I need another billing clerk. Do you know anyone who is looking for a job that could do the work? You know our standards. We need a responsible person who will fit in here. If you know of someone, please let me know."

Most likely the employee understands exactly what is wanted and will not suggest unsuitable people.

On-campus recruiting trips, too, begin with this limited selection concept. Say a recruiter for a brokerage firm contacts the state university's placement office:

> "I'm going to visit your campus next month to see about recruiting some of your students as stockbroker trainees. I would like to interview only seniors who will graduate this semester. I'm interested in those who have a B or better grade average and are majoring in finance, accounting or economics. Can you set up some interviews for the 14th? I can be there all day."

Likewise, an employment agency does the advertising, screening and initial selection to provide a limited supply of applicants, but the supply consists of only those who meet the selection criteria provided the employment firm.

The Application Form

Recruiting methods develop a pool of applicants; from this pool, the active selection process commences. Active selection refers to the process of face-to-face contact, where someone interviews the job applicant. Before this, though, all of the candidates must go through a passive pre-screening step--filling out the application form.

The design of the application form must serve two purposes. First, it provides the employer with basic job-related information on the applicant which can be used as a screening tool. Second, it must comply with Title VII of the Civil Rights Act of 1964. Application forms, because of legal restrictions, are not able to collect as much information as employers might like to have for comparing candidates.

The 1978 Uniform Guidelines on Employee Selection Procedures were adopted by the EEOC, the Civil Service Commission, the Department of Justice, and the Department of Labor to provide guidance to ensure that Title VII is complied with when selecting employees.

Title VII prohibits hiring discrimination on the basis of race, color, religion, sex, or national origin. The guidelines also provide information relative to other laws applicable to hiring procedures.

The following should be considered in the preparation of an application form or when collecting other information about prospective employees:

Name: Name only. Other aspects such as titles (Mr., Miss, Mrs.) are illegal.

Age: Any questions seeking the age or birthdate are illegal.

RECRUITING

Height or weight: Unless a Bona Fide Occupational Qualification (BFOQ), questions seeking this information are illegal.

Religion: Questions seeking religious affiliation (unless a BFOQ) cannot be asked.

Race or color: Questions on color of skin, eyes, hair, etc., are illegal as are questions on race or national origin. Requiring photographs is also illegal (prior to hiring).

Citizenship: Questions can be asked to determine if a person is a United States citizen or authorized to remain permanently in the United States. Questions cannot be asked to determine "how" a person came to be a citizen (e.g., naturalized or native).

Education: Questions may be asked to determine extent of education but not dates of education.

Military service: Questions cannot be asked regarding branch of military service or type of discharge or release from active duty.

Arrests or convictions: Unless certain crimes are related to employment conditions, questions cannot be asked regarding arrests or convictions.

Next of kin: The name, address and phone number of someone to contact in case of an emergency is legal. Requesting information about relatives (unless applicant is a minor or if relatives are employed by the company) is not legal. If the applicant prefers to list a relative as an emergency source, any relationship does not have to be listed.

Sex: Cannot be asked unless a BFOQ.

Marital status: Questions seeking marital status or information on spouses cannot be asked.

Handicaps: Questions about current or past physical limitations (unless a BFOQ) cannot be asked.

Living quarters: Questions seeking information on home ownership are also illegal.

A basic concept to keep in mind is that any information sought must be relevant to job performance, must not be seen as having a disparate impact, and must not have the potential to put the respondent in a less desirable category or classification.

An example of an employment application is found in Worksheet 8-1.

STAFFING A SMALL BUSINESS

The Recruiting Process

The recruiting process begins with the recognition of a need to develop and fill a job position. Upon determining what kind of person is needed to fill the position, recruiting sources are evaluated and selected.

Records of the different recruiting methods help companies evaluate the effectiveness (and cost) of each method (Charts 8-1 and 8-2).

All companies should also have written recruiting and hiring policies to provide guidelines for a systematic process and to ensure compliance with all federal laws and regulations.

The company should have an Equal Opportunity Statement (Chart 8-3), a Recruitment Policy Statement (Chart 8-4), and a Recruiting Procedures Guide (Chart 8-5) to provide assistance in following company policy when recruiting and selecting employees.

The most important tools to fill a job position are:

1. The job description: to define exactly what is needed.

2. The most appropriate method of advertising the position to attract the best qualified candidates.

3. The application form: to serve as a pre-screening device.

4. The job interview.

5. Tests (if appropriate): to confirm the ability to do the job.

6. Background investigation: to verify the candidate's information.

RECRUITING

Chart 8-1 Record of Recruiting Method

Recruiting source: _____Daily News (classified ads)_____

Date(s) used: _____Friday, May 27 through Sunday, May 29_____

Cost: _____$19.50_____

Position being recruited: _____Assistant Store Manager_____

Text if advertisement:
    Help Wanted   College graduate with a background in retail women's wear to be assistant store manager in large urban shopping mall. Career position, pay competitive, company benefits. Call Mr. Maxwell 555-1010 for interview appointment.

Narrative if a visit:

Number of responses: _____21_____

Comments:
    Excellent response—possibly due to timing, near college graduation.

FINAL EVALUATION: Good source - use again.

STAFFING A SMALL BUSINESS

Chart 8-2 Record of Recruiting Method

Recruiting source: <u>State College (Mr. Plant, Dir. Placement)</u>

Date(s) used: <u>Interviews mornings of Thu/Fri, May 26, 27</u>

Cost: <u>Six hours of store manager's time</u>

Position being recruited: <u>Assistant Store Manager</u>

Text if advertisement:

Narrative if a visit:

Set up interview with seven seniors to graduate in June. Four were marketing majors, two were management majors, and one general business. Four were on time and three were 5-15 minutes late.

Number of responses: _____7_____

Comments:

At this late date in the semester, it was obvious that all seven interviewees were not outstanding candidates. Five had C-averages with almost no experience. Two had adequate grade-point averages but weren't interested.

FINAL EVALUATION: Next time go earlier in the semester.

RECRUITING

Chart 8-3 Equal Opportunity Statement

Equal Opportunity

It is the policy of (company name) to implement affirmatively equal opportunity to all qualified employees and applicants for employment without regard to race, creed, color, sex, age, national origin, disability, or marital status. We will take positive action to ensure fulfillment of this policy in all areas, including hiring, placement, promotion, transfer or demotion, recruitment, employment ads, wage rates and other forms of compensation, and selection for training, layoff or termination.

This policy of (company name) is consistent with the requirements and objectives of the Civil Rights Act of 1964, the Age Discrimination Law of 1968, and all other legislation having to do with equal employment opportunities.

The objective of (company name) is to obtain individuals qualified and/or trainable for the position by virtue of job-related standards of education, training, experience, and personal qualifications.

STAFFING A SMALL BUSINESS

Chart 8-4 Sample Recruitment Policy Statement

Recruitment

The policy of (company name) is to fill job openings with the best qualified persons available, without discrimination because of race, color, creed, sex, age, national origin, disability, or marital status. Responsibility for initiating action to fill a job opening and for final selection of the person to fill that opening rests with the line organization. Executives, department heads, and others in managerial positions have the final say regarding who will work in their respective jurisdictions.

Job applicants shall be recruited as needed. Several recruiting sources used by our company include:

1. Present employees.
2. Referrals by customers and other friends of the company.
3. Newspaper advertisements.
4. Walk-in applicants.
5. Private and state employment services.
6. Reputable skill training centers.

We do not directly solicit employees of other industry firms in our market area. If an individual, currently employed by another similar organization, applies to (company name) on his or her own, we will offer him or her the same confidential treatment we do any other applicant.

All job application forms must be filled out on-site at (company name), and turned in by the applicant to the appropriate department manager.

RECRUITING

Chart 8-5 Recruiting Procedures Guide

Applicants

Recruitment is largely a quantitative function, whereas selection is qualitative. Employees must be selected from those applicants who best meet specific job requirements and who fulfill the standards of character, capacity and appearance required of all (company name) employees.

All candidates for employment will complete the company application form. After reviewing the application form, the department manager will interview the applicant and then complete the interview report form indicating his or her decision on hiring. If the candidate satisfactorily meets the department requirements, the general manager will be notified and another interview arranged with the general manager. (This may be done informally while the applicant is still at (company name).

If the two interviews suggest the candidate is acceptable, a telephone check will be made with the applicant's previous employer by the department manager. A telephone reference checksheet should be used. Depending upon the time factor and circumstances, the department manager may want written references. If so, a copy of the written request for reference should be used.

Other information needed prior to final selection (again depending upon job requirements) may be an applicant's certification license or registration and preemployment health information.

Because many jobs in our company require a current state driver's license, we are requesting that information be included in each applicant's file.

If the applicant is hired, the date and time of reporting to work and starting salary should be indicated in the remarks section of the interview report form. The starting salary should be discussed with the general manager prior to any commitment to the prospective employee.

The Civil Rights Act of 1964 requires that all applicants be considered without regard to their race, color, religion, sex, national origin, disability, or marital status. To avoid discrimination charges, managers must not ask for the following information during pre-employment interviews:

1. Age, or date and place of birth (or nationality)
2. Place of birth (or nationality) of mother, father, wife or other close relative
3. Religious affiliation (denomination, name of church, pastor, etc.)
4. Color of skin
5. Whether naturalized or native born
6. The name of any relative other than father, mother, husband or wife and minor children
7. Club, societies and lodge memberships

STAFFING A SMALL BUSINESS

8. Original name where it has been changed by court order
9. Birth certificate, naturalization or baptismal record
10. Photograph
11. Citizenship (name of country)
12. Mother tongue
13. Marital status
14. Maiden name
15. Child care arrangements

RECRUITING

Worksheet 8-1 Application for Employment

We are an equal opportunity employment company. We are dedicated to a policy of non-discrimination in employment on any basis including race, creed, color, age, sex, religion, national origin or physical defects.

Date

Personal Information

Name _____
        last   first   middle

Present address _____
      street   city   state   zip

Permanent address _____
      street   city   state   zip

Phone number   Social Security Number

Referred by

Employment Desired

Position   Date you can start   Salary desired

Are you employed now?   If so, may we inquire of your present employer?

Have you ever applied for work at this company before?

    If so, where   when

STAFFING A SMALL BUSINESS

Education

	Name and Location of School	Number of Years Attended	Indicate Diploma or Degree	Subjects Studied
Grammar School				
High School				
Trade, Business or Correspondence School				
College				
Graduate or Professional School				

Subjects of special study or research work

Did you serve in the U.S. military?

Activities other than religious (civic, athletic, fraternal, etc.)

(Exclude organizations the name or character of which indicate the race, creed, color or national origin of its members.)

RECRUITING

Former Employers (List below the last four employers, starting with the last one first)

Date Month & Year	Name and Address of Employer	Salary	Position	Reason for Leaving
From				
To				
From				
To				
From				
To				
From				
To				

References (List the names of two persons not related to you, whom you have known at least one year.)

Name	Address	Business	Years Acquainted

STAFFING A SMALL BUSINESS

Please read before signing (If you have any questions regarding this statement, please consult with a company representative before signing.)

I certify that the foregoing statements are true and correct to the best of my knowledge and belief, and hereby grant (company name) permission to verify such answers. I understand that any false statements on this application may be considered sufficient cause for rejection of this application, or for dismissal if such false statement is discovered subsequent to my employment.

If employed by (company name) , I will comply with all rules and regulations as set forth in the company's policy manual or other communications distributed to all employees. I understand that my employment is for no stated term and is subject to termination at the will of the company.

I understand that this application is void 90 days from this date.

I hereby acknowledge that I have read the above statement and understand the same.

Date _____ Signature_____

Interviewer's Comments

(This section is optional.)

Interviewer's name_____

Date of interview_____

Chapter 9
The Selection Process

Summary of Chapter

The selection process begins with the application form, which the company uses as an initial screening device when deciding who to invite for an interview.

The interview is conducted to collect more information from the applicant and to let the applicant visit the company. School or employment references may then be checked.

For certain job positions some tests (aptitude, ability, physical) may be required to determine skill levels, performance capabilities, or physical condition and abilities. Some mid-level managerial positions may call for in-depth interviews with top executives to assess the more personal qualities and compatibility of the applicant.

If the company does not reject the applicant, then it must decide if it wants to hire the person and for how much. A job offer is tendered and if the applicant accepts, the selection process has ended.

Introduction

The selection process involves gathering information about an applicant's job-related experience and skills within legal guidelines. This procedure aims to predict how the applicant will perform in a given job position. The process ends when an applicant is selected, offered a position, and accepts.

Other results of the selection process may be to reject applicants, or to find some qualified but not selected. These qualified applicants would be considered for future openings.

The process is a mutual one. At the same time the company is assessing the applicant, the applicant is deciding if he or she wants to work for the company. Both are free to terminate the process at any time.

STAFFING A SMALL BUSINESS

The Initial Screening

In the initial screening stage, the completed application form is compared against the requirements of the job. A preliminary interview may be conducted at the time the applicant submits an application. The interviewer may go over the form with the job seeker or exchange information. The interviewer may add comments to the application regarding behavior, appearance, enthusiasm, motivation, or anything else that may be of value to the person(s) doing the selection.

The initial screening will reject those who obviously do not meet the minimum job requirements. Next, the remaining applications are reviewed and the candidates ranked by their qualifications and experience.

Contacting the Applicants

It is common courtesy, though not universal business practice, to inform all applicants what the decision is regarding their application. While being too specific may invite problems, applicants can be told (assuming it is true) that they did not meet the minimum job requirements or that the person selected was better qualified for the position. People applying for jobs appreciate knowing their status as quickly as possible with some explanation.

Rather than telling an applicant he or she was rejected, try to emphasize the fact that a better qualified person was selected. It is much nicer to think that one missed out on a position because of outstanding competition rather than to feel rejected for being unqualified. A kindly versed rejection will usually draw thanks for the courteous and prompt feedback and promote the goodwill of a company.

Those who were not eliminated by the initial screening are set up for an interview.

Before the Interview. Interview scheduling can be based on the number of applicants. If a company has fifteen qualified applicants and has been able to clearly rank-order them, it might be best to interview the top five first to save time and money.

The interviewer, in a small business, should be the **manager** or **supervisor** the applicant will be working for. This means a retail store manager looking for a new sales trainee should assign the interviewing not to the sales clerk the trainee would be working under, but to the sales clerk supervisor or assistant manager responsible for the sales clerk.

Prior to seeing the applicants, the interviewer should become thoroughly familiar with their applications. The interviewer may happen to have personal connections with some aspect of the applicant's background, such as both graduating from the same school or an applicant's reference being known to the interviewer. This informal contact can be used to gather some friendly and useful information.

Types of Interviews. Determine beforehand what kind of interview to conduct.

1. **Structured or patterned.** This type of interview is based on preselected questions listed on a check sheet. It is designed to establish a uniform situation for every applicant. If time is crucial, this method ensures consistency between interviews, and time is not lost deviating from the script.

2. **Informal.** An informal interview takes place in an easy, relaxed atmosphere. Typically, it can begin with some small talk, thanking the applicant for coming, providing some general information on the position or the company, and then asking the applicant to tell about him or herself. The interviewer may have to prompt a shy applicant or maintain control with a very talkative candidate. This type of interview is not an aimless, casual social chat but like any interview should have a direction and be designed to collect specific data.

3. **Stress.** This type of interview is designed to test the ability of the applicant to withstand a potential anxiety-provoking interaction. Questions require considerable thought, knowledge or foresight; for instance, inquiring into the applicants' detailed knowledge of a complex theoretical process, asking the applicants to assess their strengths and weaknesses, or creating hypothetical situational work problems seeking how the applicant would respond and why. A stress interview is not set up to harass applicants but to evaluate their range of responses and disposition in stressful situations.

4. **Panel.** A panel interview is conducted with several people doing the interviewing. A panel interview allows several people to simultaneously and independently evaluate an applicant while observing the applicant's interactions with other people. When several people conduct an interview at the same time, much less time is required of the applicant; nevertheless a panel interview can be lengthy if all interviewers have a long list of items. Panel interviews tend to be more efficient if one person is designated to run them.

A good rule for selecting the type of interview to conduct is to pick the type that the interviewer is most comfortable with given the time available for the session.

Interviewer Preparation

Preparing for the interview is very important. The interviewer should determine what specific objectives are desired, then decide on the questions necessary to reach them. Some interviewers may prefer to concentrate on the vocational qualities of the applicant while others would rather assess the personality characteristics.

STAFFING A SMALL BUSINESS

The best way to make sure the right questions are asked is to have a list of the questions prepared before the interview. Notes may be written on this question list. Chart 9-1 contains some sample interview questions. The interview serves two purposes: the interviewer can interact personally with the applicant and can obtain more information about the applicant's background, experience, skills, and abilities. Checklists of what should be accomplished and the method to be used are vital tools for the interviewer.

The interview report is the final summary of the interview process. It allows the interviewer to rate the applicant in a variety of areas from appearance to behavior during the session to job related background. The report also contains space for comments (or a written summary). Chart 9-2 gives an example.

The interview should be conducted where it will not be interrupted. The room should comfortably hold all of the people involved. A desk or table should be available for the interviewer to spread out notes and provide a surface for writing. The overall climate of both the room and the session should be warm, open, friendly, and unhurried (unless conducting a stress interview).

Conducting the Interview

The interviewer should enjoy conversing with people. Appropriate questions must be asked to elicit appropriate responses. The interviewer must also be able to listen attentively. Chart 9-3 contains some interviewing tips.

When the objectives of the interview have been met, the interviewer should close the session. It helps if the interviewer will summarize what has been discussed and what (if any) conclusions have been reached. The applicant should be told what to expect next and when. "Don't call us, we'll call you" is not a fair way to treat an applicant. Set a specific date when the applicant will learn the outcome of the interview or the next step in the selection process.

While the job interview is the most common tool used to select workers, research has demonstrated that it is very susceptible to personal biases and misinterpretation. Its validity and reliability are not very good. But there are some things an interviewer can do to increase the validity of the interview results. Begin with a thorough knowledge of the job, the requirements to enter the position, and career progression possibilities within the job. Arrive at the interview session relaxed with a firm set of objectives in mind. Have the completed application form and checklists to refer to, to ensure that all of the appropriate areas are covered. Be aware of the following research findings:

1. Unfavorable comments are usually perceived as more critical than favorable comments. A single negative comment may outweigh several positive ones.

2. The more positions that must be filled, the better the applicants will be viewed by the interviewers.

Chart 9-1 Sample Interview Questions

1. Tell me about yourself.

2. What formal training have you had in this area?

3. What practical experience have you had in this area?

4. What are your strengths?

5. What are your limitations?

6. Why do you want to work for us?

7. Why do you want to leave your present job?

8. What do you like best about your present job?

9. What do you like least about your present job?

10. Are there any job conditions or situations that make you feel uneasy?

11. Where would you like to be in one year?

12. Where would you like to be in five years?

13. What kind of people do you get along with best?

14. What kind of people do you find most difficult to get along with?

15. What have you done in your present job that you are proudest of?

16. What do you expect to do in the position you are applying for?

17. Are there any things you do not expect to do in the position you are applying for?

18. How much money do you want to get for the position?

19. Do you have any questions of me or about our business?

STAFFING A SMALL BUSINESS

Chart 9-2 Sample Interview Report

Canyon Department Store
4400 Broadway
Canyon, Texas 78015

Applicant's Name   Janice Watkins   Date   July 20, 1987

Position applying for   Assistant Manager, Shoe Department

Interviewed by   R. Jones

Title   Manager   Department   Shoe

Rate the applicant in the following areas.

	Excellent	Above Average	Average	Below Average	Unsatisfactory
Appearance Cleanliness, grooming, attire	X				
Language Ability to communicate verbally		X			
Bearing Poise, manner, self-confidence		X			
Judgment Common sense, reasoning		X			
Leadership Ability to influence others		X			
Reliability Dependability	X				
Initiative Self-motivation		X			

THE SELECTION PROCESS

	Excellent	Above Average	Average	Below Average	Unsatisfactory
Intelligence Ability to grasp ideas & understand concepts		X			
Personality Ability to get along with others	X				
Job knowledge Understanding of job requirements	X				
Job background Prior experience in job area		X			
Overall Impression Total of all characteristics		X			

Comments: Ms. Watkins appears to be a very open, friendly and warm person. She seems very knowledgeable about the retail shoe business and has extensive supervisory and managerial experience. She would probably make an excellent assistant manager.

Overall impression was very favorable.

Signature /s/ R. Jones   Date July 20, 1987

STAFFING A SMALL BUSINESS

3. Applicants seen after an unfavorable applicant receive better evaluations.

4. An applicant who has had positive comments presented before negative comments during the selection process, will receive a better evaluation than another candidate who had the negative information presented first.

5. Some interviewers enter the session with a personal bias and spend the interview confirming their opinion.

6. Interviewers can be swayed considerably by applicant characteristics which have no relationship to a person's ability to do the job.

After the Interview

The process of evaluating each interview session should begin right after the session ends. The interviewer should check the notes to see that all the information needed is properly recorded. At this time, some additional comments may be added regarding appearance, how the interviewee conducted him or herself, or some interviewer impressions. Then the session can be reviewed mentally, and both the positive and negative aspects considered.

A reexamination of the notes should help to arrive at an overall conclusion regarding the applicant. This final evaluation should be written as a summary of the interview. The interviewer is now ready for another candidate.

Background and Reference Check

A background and reference check is conducted for two reasons: to verify the information provided by the applicant and to obtain impressions or opinions from other people who know the applicant.

There are several ways to do this. One is for the applicant to have reference information sent directly to the company. College and university transcripts are commonly sent from the Registrar's Office. Letters of recommendation may also be sent without passing through the applicant's hands.

A second method is for the company to mail a recommendation or reference form to the references, who are asked in a cover letter (Chart 9-4) to fill out the form and mail it back to the company. The form (Chart 9-5) usually begins by inquiring about the type and longevity of the applicant's and reference's relationship. Next, the reference is asked to rate personality or work characteristics on a three or five point scale. The final section is for written comments about the applicant. A different cover letter (Chart 9-6) and a special form should be used when soliciting information from an applicant's former (or present) employer (Chart 9-7).

THE SELECTION PROCESS

Chart 9-3 Interviewing Tips

1. **Common Interview Problems**

    o Failing to have a system so all job applicants are interviewed the same.

    o Deciding for or against an interviewee too early in the session due to his or her physical appearance, mannerisms, or other characteristics.

    o Failing to conduct a balanced interview to seek information relevant to all aspects of the job.

    o Selection decisions which were influenced by time pressures or the number of applicants interviewed.

    o The interviewer's lack of knowledge about the job position available.

    o Failure to collect sufficient information for making an employment decision.

2. **What Information Is Needed**

    o What previous experience or education has the applicant had which relates to the available job position?

    o What are the vocational objectives of the applicant?

    o Why does the applicant want to work for this company?

    o How familiar is the applicant with this company and the position he or she is seeking?

    o Why does the applicant think he or she should be hired? What contributions can be made to the company by the applicant?

    o How much money does the applicant want to earn? Why?

    o If the applicant is currently employed, why is he or she seeking a different job?

3. **How to Phrase Specific Questions**

    o You may inquire into the applicant's willingness to work the company's regular work schedule but you cannot inquire about specific religious holidays.

    o You may ask where the applicant lives but not where he or she was born.

    o You may inquire if the applicant is between 18 and 70 years old but you cannot ask the applicant's age.

    o You may ask if the applicant is a United States citizen but you cannot ask how the applicant became a citizen.

STAFFING A SMALL BUSINESS

- o You may inquire about any physical or mental disabilities which inhibit or endanger job performance but you cannot ask general medical questions.

- o You may inquire about any foreign languages the applicant speaks, reads, or writes, but you may not ask how that skill was acquired.

4. The Right (and Wrong) Way to Ask Questions

- o Ask open-ended questions which require explanations rather than those which require a yes or no.

    Example: "Tell me about your work experience with an IBM personal computer." Not "Have you ever used an IBM personal computer?"

- o Ask questions that relate to the job being applied for. Avoid personal questions that are not job related.

    Example: "Would you have any problems with working one night a week?" Not "What will your spouse say if you worked one night a week?"

- o Assume a relaxed conversational posture. Put the applicant at ease. Control the session, but do not be overbearing, demanding or defensive. Allow the applicant to respond. Make reflective comments which encourage the applicant to continue talking.

    Example: When the applicant mentions an interest in the outdoors, a reflective comment might be "You like to work outdoors." This should elicit an affirmative response and continued dialogue from the applicant.

- o Do not force the applicant to take a defensive posture by asking judgmental questions. Keep the questions as open ended and positive as possible.

    Example: "Tell me why you would like to work for our company." Not "So you want to quit your present job? How do I know you won't just quit us?"

- o Allow the applicant to respond at his or her own pace. Do not overload the person with several questions at the same time. Give the applicant the opportunity to clarify statements.

    Example : "You have heard good things about our sales force, why do you think you would enjoy working here?" Not "What have you heard about our sales force? Who told you? Do you believe it? Why do you want to work here? Do you think you will be a good sales trainee?"

A third way to do the background and reference check is to telephone the references. It could take considerable time to reach the reference; on the other hand, once the contact is established the check can be conducted very quickly. If the reference makes a statement that is ambiguous, the interviewer can ask for some additional information right then. People also tend to say more over a phone than they would in a written recommendation. The telephone verification should be carried out systematically, preferably by using a telephone reference checklist (see Chart 9-8) for phone contacts. Special forms are used for phone contacts with present or past employers (Charts 9-9 and 9-10).

Testing the Applicant

Applicant testing covers a variety of assessment and evaluation techniques. To be legal, any evaluation system used must be related to job performance. Any method of testing job applicants must have data to prove that the test is both valid and reliable. A valid test does what it is supposed to, that is, it measures what it is designed to measure. A reliable test is consistent in what it measures. It must do what it is designed to do every time.

Another aspect of validity and reliability in testing is standardization: the test must be given every time under the same conditions and circumstances. The methods used, the sequential order of the testing if it consists of more than one part, the instructions to the test taker, and the setting in which the testing is conducted must always be the same. Any deviation could affect the test's reliability, even its validity

Another concept of employment testing is fairness. If a particular segment of the population does consistently better or worse on the test, then it is not a fair evaluation. Test fairness is outlined in the Uniform Guidelines on Employment Selection Procedures. It refers to a test as being unfair, for example, if minority groups receive scores which predict lower levels of job performance than the group actually demonstrates on the job.

Common Texts

More common to small businesses are performance tests such as typing or driving tests, aptitude or skill tests in which the applicant completes a paper and pencil evaluation, and physical performance tests such as carrying a toolbox up a ladder, moving heavy containers, or maneuvering in close quarters. Many occupations require specific physical abilities: mechanics, fire fighters, sanitation workers, exterior window washers, and carpenters may be some examples.

Some tests consist of duplicating certain performance of job behaviors in a test setting and having the applicant demonstrate that he or she can perform as

STAFFING A SMALL BUSINESS

Chart 9-4 Written Request for Reference

Canyon Department Store
4400 Broadway
Canyon, Texas 79015

Date   July 20, 1987

Mr. Roy Redmond
1246 Wilson Drive
Canyon, TX 79015

Dear Mr. Redmond:

Ms. Janice Watkins has applied at our store for employment as Assistant Manager, Shoe Department and has given us your name as a reference. Would you please complete the attached form and return it to us in the self-addressed envelope at your earliest convenience.

                        Thank you

                        /s/ Ralph Jones

                        Ralph Jones,
                        Manager
                        Shoe Department

THE SELECTION PROCESS

Chart 9-5 Reference Form

Canyon Department Store
4400 Broadway
Canyon, Texas 79015

Reference for ____Ms. Janice Watkins_____

I have known this person as a:
    ____Neighbor
    ____Fellow worker
    ____Personal friend
    ____Acquaintance
    __•Family friend
    ____Other_____

I have known this person for _____ years.

Do you want this person to see these remarks?
Yes ____ No ____

Please rate the individual in the following areas:

	Excellent	Above Average	Average	Below Average	Unsatisfactory
Appearance Cleanliness, grooming, attire					
Language Ability to communicate verbally					
Bearing Poise, manner, self-confidence					
Judgment Common sense, reasoning					
Leadership Ability to influence others					
Reliability Dependability					
Initiative Self-motivation					
Intelligence Ability to grasp ideas & understand concepts					

STAFFING A SMALL BUSINESS

	Excellent	Above Average	Average	Below Average	Unsatisfactory

Personality
  Ability to get
  along with others					

Overall Impression
  Total of all
  characteristics					

Please provide any additional information to help us better understand how he or she will be an asset to our business.

_____
Signature   Date

_____
Your name

Address

Occupation

Position/Title

THE SELECTION PROCESS

Chart 9-6 Request for Reference from Previous Employer

                      Canyon Department Store
                            4400 Broadway
                        Canyon, Texas 79015

                                  July 20, 1987

Ms. Helen White
Manager, Shoe Department
Acme Clothing Store
25 Main Street
Canyon, TX 79015

Dear Ms. White:

Ms. Janice Watkins has applied at our store for employment as Assistant Manager, Shoe Department and has stated that she was in your employ from January 5, 1982, to present in the capacity of Sales Clerk Supervisor, Shoe Department.

Please complete the enclosed form and return it to us in the self-addressed envelope at your earliest convenience.

                                  Thank you

                                  /s/ R. Jones
                                  Ralph Jones
                                  Manager
                                  Shoe Department

STAFFING A SMALL BUSINESS

Chart 9-7 Sample Previous Employer Reference Form

Canyon Department Store
4400 Broadway
Canyon, Texas 79015

Name _____
Date of Employment _____ Date of Termination _____
Position Held _____
Reason for Termination _____
Please check the appropriate column indicating your rating of the applicant.

	Excellent	Above Average	Average	Below Average	Unsatisfactory	Unable to Evaluate
Technical ability						
Attendance record						
Ability to get along with others						
Cooperation						
Appearance						
Ability to take instructions						
Common sense						
Effective utilization of time						

Any injury on the job? _____ If yes, please state date, nature, lost time.

Would you re-employ? Yes ____ No ____ If not, why?

Do you recommend the applicant?

Additional remarks:

Date   Signed
                        Title

THE SELECTION PROCESS

Chart 9-8 Telephone Reference Check

Canyon Department Store
4400 Broadway
Canyon, Texas 79015

Name of Applicant____Janice Watkins____Date____July 20, 1985____
Reference name____Roy Redmond____Phone____255-0048____
Relationship to applicant____Family banker____

Telephone reference checking is the fastest and many times the most informative method of learning about your applicant's history and abilities. Verify the facts given on the personnel application. Call person-to-person to the applicant's references. These could include landlord, last immediate supervisor, business associates, school authorities, or other person the applicant has listed as a reference.

Suggested wording for starting your conversation

Mr.
Mrs.
Ms.____Redmond____(reference) this is____Ralph Jones (interviewer)____.
I'm calling to verify information provided to us by____Janice Watkins (applicant), who has authorized us to discuss this with you.

Mr./Mrs./Ms.____Watkins____has given us your name as a reference on his/her application for employment with the Canyon Department Store. Would you mind answering some questions on his/her behalf?

Is the applicant known to you personally? Yes__x__ No___

Is the applicant known to you professionally? Yes__x__ No___

How long have you known the applicant?____since birth____

What is the nature of your acquaintance with the applicant?

I have been the family banker with the Watkins family for 30 years. I have known Janice since she was born. She is a very intelligent, hard working young lady who has always been reliable and dependable. In her present position she probably has no chance for promotion because no one is expected to leave.

Thank you for your assistance.

STAFFING A SMALL BUSINESS

Chart 9-9 Telephone Reference Check from Previous Employer

Canyon Department Store
4400 Broadway
Canyon, Texas 79015

Name of applicant___Janice Watkins___ Date___July 20, 1987___

Mr.
Mrs.
Ms.___White___ (Reference), this is___Ralph Jones (interviewer), Manager of the Shoe Department at Canyon Department Store___. I'm calling to verify information provided by___Janice Watkins (applicant)___who has authorized us to discuss this with you. Mr./Mrs./Ms.___Watkins (applicant)___has given us your name on his/her application for employment with our organization. Would you mind answering some questions on his/her behalf?

In reference to applicant's job/school work, what was the nature of the work or studies:___Sales Clerk___

Did the applicant carry out this work satisfactorily? Yes _x_ No ___

Did the applicant advance in his/her position? Yes _x_ No ___

How does applicant get along with associates, customers, supervisors? ___Very well. She is a very friendly person and liked by everyone.___

Does applicant follow instructions satisfactorily? Yes _x_ No ___

Does applicant lose any time because of poor health? Yes ___ No _x_

Is the applicant dependable and reliable? ___Yes, always___

Does the applicant possess leadership abilities? ___Yes, very much so___

Do you think the applicant would fit in with our company?
Yes _x_ No ___

Do you have any other comments on his/her work behavior or why he/she is looking for employment elsewhere?

She is an excellent worker. Unfortunately, we do not expect any vacancies to open in a managerial position so we are unable to offer Janice the promotion she deserves.

Thank you for your assistance.

THE SELECTION PROCESS

Chart 9-10 Telephone Reference Check from Previous Employer

Canyon Department Store
4400 Broadway
Canyon, Texas 79015

Applicant's name ____Janice Watkins____ Date ____July 20, 1987____

Company name ____Acme Clothing Store____ Telephone ____555-3031____

Dates of Employment ____January 5, 1982____ To ____Present____

Position and Title ____Sales Clerk Supervisor____

Duties: Assists manager in supervising all Shoe Department sales clerks, trains new clerks, responsible for conduct of sales clerks, handles complaints from customers, conducts sales in Shoe Department.

Reason for leaving: 1No vacancies for promotion available at this time.

How would you rate the employee's performance? ____excellent____

Were there any problems with absenteeism? ____none____

How did the applicant get along with others? ____extremely well____

Applicant states earnings were ____$14,000 per year____

If not, correct amount $ _____

Would you rehire? Yes __x__ No ____

Additional comments: We would like to keep Janice but she deserves a managerial position and we have none available and foresee no openings in the near future.

Information received from ____Helen White____

Title ____Manager, Shoe Department____

Date ____July 20, 1985____

Received by ____R. Jones, Manager, Shoe Department____

required. These tests measure a person's ability to replicate the physical maneuvers necessary for adequate job performance. The tests may evaluate general areas such as manual dexterity, strength, gross motor coordination, or physical agility. Other tests may examine specific areas such as the ability to perform real work tasks in simulated work environments such as disassembling or assembling machines or motors, sorting mail, or working cash registers.

All of these tests measure an applicant's ability to respond physically as required on the actual job.

Assessment Centers

Some businesses that require a high degree of technical proficiency may use vocational assessment centers to evaluate job applicants. Assessment centers are staffed by trained professionals who conduct evaluations in a highly scientific manner, collecting data in a specific manner in a controlled environment. This process can be very expensive and require several days for the assessment. Assessment centers may also be used to evaluate candidates for top corporate executive positions.

Medical Examinations

Medical examinations may be used to detect physical conditions that may be subject to aggravation on the job (heart disease, for instance) or to assure that certain physical characteristics of the applicant fall within established limits (e.g., visual or auditory acuity). These are becoming more accepted as the cost of litigation for job-related physical aggravation increases.

Many businesses ask applicants to complete a pre-employment health information questionnaire (Chart 9-11). The form protects the company as much as it does the applicant if hired. Any listed impairments should be medically evaluated relative to job performance prior to employment.

Unlike other types of testing, most physical examinations require the services of a physician licensed to practice medicine within the state. The question of the doctor-patient relationship arises when the physician is hired by a business and not the patient. To whom is the physician responsible? The conduct of medical practice is regulated by each state, so the legal implications surrounding pre-employment medical examinations must be determined within the confines of each state.

Chart 9-11 Pre-Employment Health Information Questionnaire

Canyon Department Store
4400 Broadway
Canyon, Texas 79015

Name __Janice Watkins__

Address __1127 Conrad Avenue, Canyon, TX 79015__

Telephone number __555-9780__

Position applied for __Assistant Manager, Shoe Department__

Please list any impairments—physical or mental—that would interfere with your ability to perform in the position named above. If none, write none.

    None

Are there any job duties you cannot perform because of a physical handicap? Yes___ No _x_ . If yes, please explain.

Are there any other positions or types of positions for which you should not be considered because of a physical handicap? Yes___ No _x_ . If yes, please explain.

I have read the above questions and answered them to the best of my knowledge.

Signed __/s/ Janice Watkins__   Date __July 27, 1987__

STAFFING A SMALL BUSINESS

Testing and Evaluation Summary

Managers and employers should heed this advice: any testing utilized must be a valid predictor of specific job performance. The ability to develop tests that conform to the criteria of the Uniform Guidelines on Employment Selection Procedures is probably beyond the capability of most managers. For this reason managers must know where to go to obtain tests that are legal.

Industrial and organizational psychologists are the primary source for information regarding pen and paper or ability performance tests. Questions on medical examinations should be addressed to the local medical society. Both professions have a licensing agency at the state level which can provide assistance. The American Psychological Association and the American Medical Association provide guidelines to their members in their respective areas of pre-employment testing.

Deciding Who to Hire

After all the applications have been sifted, interviews conducted, and testing completed, a decision on which candidate to hire is made based on the accumulated information.

Each step of the selection process may serve as part of a "go or no-go" system. The job candidate who fails to meet or exceed any one of the standards during the selection process may be terminated immediately as a potential employee. This concept has both advantages and disadvantages. The major advantage is the savings to a company in time and money, especially if there are many applicants. On the other hand, there is the danger of prematurely disqualifying an excellent candidate. In many cases the full value of an applicant may not be recognized until he or she has completed the entire selection process. Because early termination may unjustly eliminate a highly qualified prospect, some companies consider all applicants that survive the initial screening until one of the applicants accepts a job offer.

The selection process should gather information that determines which applicant will best perform the job. The final decision should be based on an honest appraisal of the experience, abilities, and skills of each one, and a fair match between what the job requires and what each candidate could do in the job. Personal preferences, likes or dislikes, must be recognized and put aside if an evaluation is to be fair.

The selection process, if conducted properly by an individual who knows what to look for, can lead to successfully recognizing the talent which will serve the company best--and who is second best, third best, and so on. Once the decision is reached, a job offer can be extended to the top applicant.

Presenting the Job Offer

Do not assume that the best candidate will accept: someone else may also be wanting his or her services. The acceptance of the job offer may depend upon certain employment conditions being negotiated. Duties, pay, benefits, hours, vacations, titles, or responsibilities may be areas of contention in which compromise can occur.

Both employer and job candidate should clearly understand those areas in which some negotiation is acceptable. If an area is not negotiable, then this must be clearly stated at the outset. A promising employee-employer relationship can disintegrate in a matter of minutes because of misunderstanding. Make sure to know if everything is clearly understood regarding employment conditions, or if there are still areas to be decided. If all conditions are already agreed upon then present the job offer as understood. When no negotiations are required, all that is needed is a yes or no.

If there are contractual areas yet to be settled, it is important to have a clear idea of what the candidate wants to negotiate for. Salary, areas of responsibility, and other aspects of employment should have been discussed earlier, during the selection process; still, in many cases the final aspects of duties and compensation are truly dependent on the candidate's experience and qualifications.

Enter negotiations with a clear concept of what the candidate is worth to the company and do not exceed that. If the candidate's demands clearly exceed this limit, terminate the negotiations, thank the candidate for his or her participation and interest, and begin to talk to the second ranked candidate.

Do not become forced to over-compensate because all other alternative candidates have been terminated. The company that still has alternative choices is in good shape, but the company that has put all of its bets on one person who declines probably has to repeat most of the selection process. When someone has been told that a job has been filled and is asked later to assume that same position, both the company and the applicant may feel uncomfortable. Thus it is advisable not to eliminate any acceptable candidates until the position is actually filled.

The selection process can be a complex, time-consuming procedure for both employer and applicants. Successful candidates are not the result of a haphazard process; quality comes from a system that understands what is needed and how to fill that need. Quality candidates are the result of a system that has clearly defined job descriptions, attracts the best available applicants, is competitive in the compensation offered, and does a thorough job of individually evaluating each applicant. Success begets success.

THE SELECTION PROCESS

Worksheet 9-1 Interview Report

Applicant's Name _____ Date _____

Position applying for _____

Interviewed by_____

Title _____ Department _____

Rate the applicant in the following areas.

	Excellent	Above Average	Average	Below Average	Unsatisfactory
Appearance Cleanliness, grooming, attire					
Language Ability to communicate verbally					
Bearing Poise, manner, self-confidence					
Judgment Common sense, reasoning					
Leadership Ability to influence others					
Reliability Dependability					
Initiative Self-motivation					

STAFFING A SMALL BUSINESS

	Excellent	Above Average	Average	Below Average	Unsatisfactory
Intelligence Ability to grasp ideas & understand concepts					
Personality Ability to get along with others					
Job knowledge Understanding of job requirements					
Job background Prior experience in job area					
Overall Impression Total of all characteristics					

Comments:

Signature _____ Date _____

Worksheet 9-2 Telephone Reference Check from Previous Employer

Name of Applicant   Date

Reference name   Phone

Relationship to applicant

Suggested wording for starting your conversation

Mr.
Mrs.
Ms. (reference) this is (interviewer). I'm calling to verify information provided to us by (applicant), who has authorized us to discuss this with you.

Mr./Mrs./Ms._____ has given us your name as a reference on his/her application for employment with _____. Would you mind answering some questions on his/her behalf?

Is the applicant known to you personally? Yes ___ No ___

Is the applicant known to you professionally? Yes ___ No ___

How long have you known the applicant? _____

What is the nature of your acquaintance with the applicant?

Thank you for your assistance.

STAFFING A SMALL BUSINESS

Worksheet 9-3 Telephone Reference Check from Previous Employer

Name of applicant_____ Date _____
Mr.
Mrs.
Ms. _____ (reference), this is (interviewer), (position), (department), (company).

I'm calling to verify information provided by _____ (applicant) who has authorized us to discuss this with you.

Mr./Mrs./Ms. _____ (applicant) has given us your name on his/her application for employment with our organization.

Would you mind answering some questions on his/her behalf? In reference to applicant's job/school work, what was the nature of the work or studies:

Did the applicant carry out this work satisfactorily? Yes___ No___

Did the applicant advance in his/her position? Yes___ No___

How does applicant get along with associates, customers, supervisors?

Does applicant follow instructions satisfactorily? Yes___ No___

Does applicant lose any time because of poor health? Yes___ No___

Is the applicant dependable and reliable?

Does the applicant possess leadership abilities?

Do you think the applicant would fit in with our company?
    Yes___ No___

Do you have any other comments on his/her work behavior or why he/she is looking for employment elsewhere?

Thank you for your assistance.

Worksheet 9-4 Telephone Reference Check from Previous Employer

Applicant's name_____ Date_____

Company name_____ Telephone_____

Dates of Employment_____ To_____

Position and Title_____
_____

Duties:

_____

Reason for leaving:

How would you rate the employee's performance?

Were there any problems with absenteeism?

How did the applicant get along with others?

Applicant states earnings were

If not, correct amount

Would you rehire? Yes____ No ____ If not, reason:

_____

Additional comments:

_____

Information received from_____

Title_____

Date_____

Received by_____

_____

STAFFING A SMALL BUSINESS

Worksheet 9-5 Pre-Employment Health Information Questionnaire

Name
_____

Address
_____

Telephone number
_____

Position applied for
_____

Please list any impairments--physical or mental--that would interfere with your ability to perform in the position named above. If none, write none.

_____

Are there any job duties you cannot perform because of a physical handicap?

    Yes____ No____

    If yes, please explain.

_____

Are there any other positions or types of positions for which you should not be considered because of a physical handicap?

    Yes____ No____

    If yes, please explain.

_____

I have read the above questions and answered them to the best of my knowledge.

Signed_____ Date_____
_____

Chapter 10

Placement in the Company

Summary of Chapter

This chapter is a guide to orienting a new employee to a business. The orientation begins with the company's perspective of the organization and ends with an introduction to the employee's particular job setting and overseeing the new worker's first efforts.

An employee who knows exactly what is expected of him or her and the rules governing these expectations should be better able to concentrate on doing what he or she was hired for. The more complete the orientation process, the quicker the new employee can become a valuable member of the organization.

Introduction

The company orientation is too often seen by managers (and many employees) as a necessary rite of passage, from applicant to employee that should be accomplished as rapidly as possible. The truth is, this transformation should be carefully planned and executed to properly (and favorably) introduce a new hire into the business. Its success will be limited unless the inductee learns what the company rules, regulations, policies, and career opportunities are. Orientation into a business is both a passive and active process. The passive part involves the employee handbook: the written information provided to help the new hire understand the company, the rewards and benefits it provides, and his or her obligations to the company. The active part involves escorting the new employee to meet and talk to various people in the company who are important to that person's assimilation into the company. Each part complements the other. A business that does not offer both does not offer new employees a complete orientation.

The Employee Handbook

The purpose of the handbook is to provide each employee with a printed copy of the organization's policies and practices. It serves as a guide for routine procedures that govern employees' day-to-day activities and behavior. It also includes information on pay, work schedules, benefits, vacations and holidays, and other options available to employees. This helps to ensure that standard policies and procedures will be understood and complied with by all employees. Managers and employees alike will have a single reference source to know what guidelines apply in most typical situations.

The employee handbook is a condensed version of the company policy and personnel manual (see **A Company Policy and Personnel Workbook** by A. R. Ramey and R. A Mrozek, 1985, Oasis Press), which is designed primarily to serve as a guide of standard operating procedures for company officers and managers. The employee handbook outlines acceptable and unacceptable behaviors as they affect the business. Managers recognize that the handbook facilitates decision making because its information is uniformly available to all employees.

An employee handbook may consist of only two or three pages containing basic rules and regulations. More pages may be used for information such as company procedures, benefits, and employee performance guidelines.

Guidelines on Developing an Employee Handbook

Policies that are in writing tend to be understood and implemented more uniformly than those that are communicated to employees verbally. Policies should be broad enough to apply in a variety of common situations, yet be specific enough to have a meaningful application to the business and the employees.

The policies and procedures should also be flexible enough to cover atypical situations appropriately, yet allow common sense to prevail as the occasion arises. Simplicity and comprehension need to be built into the handbook if it is to become a useful management tool: if no one understands just what it says, it has no value. A clear, logical format should be used at all times.

The author of the handbook must keep in mind that its purpose is to communicate to both management and employees what is expected in certain situations. If it is too elementary, it may lack the information needed to provide proper guidance; too wordy or complex and no one will use it. A balance must be maintained between simplicity and complexity to create a handbook that reinforces in writing the philosophy of the business, the objectives to be attained, and how the firm's employees should conduct themselves to achieve these objectives.

What an Employee Handbook May Contain

The following items are only a guide; each business would change, delete or substitute to suit its own requirements. (Chart 10-1 is a detailed outline.)

1. **Background.** A short history of the company sets forth basic philosophy,

PLACEMENT IN THE COMPANY

mission, purpose, and goals to provide the reader with an understanding of what the company wants to achieve.

2. **Employment** rules and regulations. Information on hiring practices, new hire orientation, assignments, and procedures for transfers, promotions, and leaves, is provided.

3. **Employee evaluations.** Job descriptions, their usage, and job performance evaluations are explained.

4. **Pay.** Wage and salary ranges, pay periods and pay procedures, how attendance is kept for pay purposes, overtime, vacation and holiday pay, and separation pay are discussed.

5. **Benefits.** Benefits available, eligibility, costs, and options are described. The typical benefits such as social security, workers' compensation, and group insurance are covered as well as holidays, vacations, and special benefits.

6. **Employee-management relations.** Information is provided on morale building, the reciprocal activities between employees and the company, and how an employee with personal or family problems may seek advice or assistance from the company.

7. **Employee safety.** Rules' and regulations applicable to employee safety are covered.

8. **General policies and procedures.** This gives guidelines of employee conduct: what behavior is required and what is prohibited during company time.

9. **Career opportunities.** The means available for career advancement are presented; requirements for promotion are explained as well as technical or educational development opportunities.

Company Orientation

The employee handbook is an effective guide for orienting new employees. The purpose of orientation is to reduce "new job anxiety" by carefully and clearly explaining what the new employee needs to know to fit in. Research reveals that inadequate orientation programs are tied to high employee turnover. The better prepared employees are to assume a position, the less likely they are to feel out of place and seek employment elsewhere.

Some orientations are informal sessions where a supervisor or manager explains all aspects of the company, personnel procedures, and introduction to the place or section where the new person will work. Other orientations consist of a program of speakers, films, and guided tours. Whichever approach is used, the key to success is to have a uniform format so that all areas are covered in the same way each time.

STAFFING A SMALL BUSINESS

Chart 10-1 Employee Handbook Outline

I. Company Background
   History of the Company
   Company Philosophy
   Mission - Purpose
   Company Goals
   How Each Employee Fits In

II. Employment Rules and Regulations
   Equal Opportunity
   Request for Personnel
   Recruitment Procedures
   Applicant Processing Procedures
   Newly Hired Employees Orientation
   Probationary Period
   Full-time Employees/Part-time Employees
   Transfers
   Promotions
   Separations
   Maternity Leave
   Military Leave (Reserve Service)

III. Employee Evaluations
   Job Descriptions
   Job Evaluation Procedures
   Employee Records
   Employee Performance Appraisal

IV. Pay
   Wage and Salary Ranges
   Payroll Records
   Change of Status
   Timekeeping
   Attendance
   Work Scheduling
   Shift Differentials
   Overtime
   Holiday Pay
   Separation Pay

PLACEMENT IN THE COMPANY

V. Benefits
       Group Insurance Plans
       Social Security
       Workers' Compensation Insurance
       Rest Breaks
       Vacations/Holidays
       Sick Leave
       Service Recognition
       Education Programs

VI. Employee-Management Relations
       Employee Advancement Opportunities
       Morale Building Programs
       Employee Counseling
       Employee Discipline
       Employee Complaints

VII. Employee Safety
       Safety and Accident Prevention
       Safety Rules and Regulations

VIII. General Policies and Procedures
       Bulletin Board
       Community Relations
       Customers
       Drug/Alcohol Abuse
       Employee Deaths
       Employee Parking
       Employee Relations
       Gifts and Entertainment
       Jury Duty
       No Solicitation -- No Distribution Policy
       Seniority
       Smoking
       Supplier Relations
       Telephone and Mail Usage
       Uniforms
       Visitors in Work Area
       Working Conditions

IX. Career Opportunities
       Promotions to Supervisory Positions
       Training and Development
       Future Considerations

STAFFING A SMALL BUSINESS

A typical company orientation should include a brief explanation of the company history, its purpose, and where it is going. It would be helpful if the person conducting the orientation could explain how the new employee's position relates to the overall operations of the company. A tour of the company facilities is important to present an overview of how the entire business operates.

The next part of the orientation is a thorough briefing on pay and benefit options and procedures. Tax forms, insurance forms, personnel forms, and other paperwork are completed at this time. Then, the employee goes to his or her workplace for the job orientation.

Job Orientation

The job orientation is the introduction to the duties that the new employee will be performing and to the place where the new employee will be working. It should be conducted by the person who the employee will be working for or the supervisor of the work unit. The most important aspect of the job orientation is to acquaint the new employee with the specific procedures involved in the job and the equipment or machinery he or she will operate. It should also include a review of the daily routine; when to report for work, when breaks can be taken, how much time may be taken for lunch, and when the workday ends.

Checklists can be a valuable tool during the orientation process. Chart 10-2 contains instructions for a supervisor on how to conduct the orientation, and Chart 10-3 is a checklist to use during orientation. Finally, a sample checklist for giving job instructions is in Chart 10-4. These should help the supervisor to conduct a complete introduction to what the company expects from the new employee.

One last item, which may not be applicable to all jobs, is the completion of a health questionnaire. Like many other aspects of personnel management, this is a precaution to prevent future health problems. Because of the potential discriminatory aspects of a health questionnaire, it should be clearly related to the potential job health hazards. Preparing one should be done with the advice of an industrial physician.

The supervisory relationships should be clearly explained so the new person will know exactly who to report to. Initial work assignments should be clearly explained. The supervisor should maintain a close watch on the new employee to see that there are no problems and that assimilation into the workforce is going smoothly.

It is important that this close supervision be done tactfully. The impression to be conveyed to employees is concern for their orientation, not distrust or too parental an attitude. As assimilation progresses, the supervisor can begin to back off. The new employee should perceive the supervisor as an interested person, ready to help as required, not someone just waiting to point out a mistake.

PLACEMENT IN THE COMPANY

Chart 10-2 Supervisor's Instructions for New Employee Orientation

The information and instructions given a new employee on his or her first day in the company go a long way in molding that person's impression of our company as an employer. To help us do a better and more thorough job of briefing new employees, an orientation checklist with new employee data form and job instruction checklist are used. Copies are attached.

The orientation checklist and data form, when completed in the department and returned to personnel, become a part of the new employee's permanent records. The form is to be completed during the first day of employment if possible. The various check points do not represent all the supervisor might want to go over with a new employee, but they serve as a guide and outline to work from.

Obtaining the employee's signature, indicating that these points have been explained to him or her, is very important. It verifies what points have been covered during the orientation.

The job instruction checklist can be used to assist in outlining the employee's job duties. Or, it can be given to whomever in your department is responsible for training or supervising the new employee as a how-we-want-it-done guide.

Depending on the job requirements, the new employee health information sheet should also be completed on the first day of work. Forward it to personnel to be included in the new employee's permanent records.

STAFFING A SMALL BUSINESS

Chart 10-3 New Employee Orientation Checklist

Part I. Orientation Checklist

Name of Employee   Date

This checklist should be completed by the employee's supervisor during the orientation process.

__ Welcome the new employee and introduce him or her to fellow workers.

__ Explain the purpose and function of the work section.

__ Describe the chain of command, work relationships, and who the employee should seek to ask questions about the job.

__ Briefly explain the department's relationship to other departments.

__ Walk the employee through the work area pointing out employee bulletin board, lockers, rest rooms, break areas, etc.

__ Review the new employee's particular job:

  __ Explain the job description.

  __ Ensure that employee knows who his or her immediate supervisor is.

  __ Briefly explain the purpose of the job.

  __ Briefly explain training period.

__ Review the company policy regarding attendance and absenteeism, and how he or she should notify the company regarding emergencies or sickness.

__ Explain policies covering work breaks and lunch periods. For the first few days ask a regular employee to accompany the new employee on breaks and lunch period.

__ Review those aspects of company policy that specifically pertain to the work habits within the work section.

Employee's signature   Date

Supervisor's signature   Date

Department Manager's Signature   Date

PLACEMENT IN THE COMPANY

Part II New Employee Data Form

This form should be completed for each new employee. Its primary purpose is to provide documentation that all employment procedures and records have been completed.

Section 1 (To be completed by department manager)

Name   Date of employment

Department   Job title

Salary   Grade

Social Security Number   Withholding status

Name of employee replaced

Check when applicable:

  New hire __   Rehire __   Permanent __   Temporary __

  Full-time __   Part-time __   Hourly __

Section 2 (To be completed by personnel department)
  __Withholding certificate W-4
  __Application
  __References
  __Licenses, registration certifications
  __Health information/physical examination
  __Fidelity bond, signature witnessed (where applicable)
  __Tests
  __Photograph
  __Insurance: Enrollment card __ Waiver card __
      Group enrollment card __ Group waiver card __

Signed   Date

STAFFING A SMALL BUSINESS

Chart 10-4 Job Instruction Checklist

Prepare:

- o Have the work space or desk clean and work materials neatly arranged as you want the new person to keep them. Have available any written instructions, training outlines, samples, or job breakdowns that may be helpful to you or the new employee.

- o Review the job duties and requirements briefly and explain how the new person will be taught. Discuss the work objectives and their relation to the department and company.

- o Emphasize your interest in helping the new person do a good job. Create interest and enthusiasm for the work. Do not stress difficulties at the beginning. Avoid technical language unless required.

Explain and Demonstrate:

- o Break down the work into readily understood steps. Take up one point at a time.

- o Tell what each step is and show how it is done. Stress key points and give reasons.

- o Be sure to explain where the work comes from and what is going to be done with it when finished.

Have Employee Explain and Demonstrate:

- o Check the employee's knowledge of each step or point by having him or her do it.

- o Have him or her tell you and show you what he or she is doing and why.

- o Correct errors promptly and constructively. Repeat your instructions as often as necessary.

Have Employee Practice:

- o When you think the employee knows enough to do the work, let him or her proceed alone.

- o Observe, coach, and correct as needed. Be quick with compliments; continually encourage by reporting progress.

Check Results and Follow-up:

- o Show an interest in the new employee and his or her work while gradually tapering off close observation and instruction.

- o Don't wait for questions--often a new employee will not ask questions. Instead, schedule time to deal with any questions.

Career Patterns

Career patterns allow employees to grow and develop within the business. Some businesses cannot do this; small businesses which are owner-managed have employees as support personnel with no advancement opportunities. Still, there are options available even in these small businesses.

First, the support personnel may outgrow their present position and use this as a stepping stone to join a larger business with more career potential. The owner-manager must recognize this situation and realize that career-oriented employees will eventually move on. This can actually be part of the incentive for new employees, that their training and experience will enhance employability in a larger organization. Another incentive can be the contacts to be made to obtain another position with more responsibility.

The second option is not always possible but certainly can happen. A support position employee over time may become so knowledgeable and valuable that the business can afford to expand. Essentially, this may create a new position for the employee to move into.

It is not uncommon for a clerk, secretary, or shop worker to become such an asset to the business that they are asked to become a junior partner. Many company presidents began as a support person (or part-time employee) and eventually worked their way into the top position. Several companies which began as a small family enterprise have endured over time because a dedicated employee displayed both the desire and ability to continue the business when family members declined to do so.

A more common way to rise in a business is for sufficient positions to be available within the organization to provide a career pattern from entry level positions to top management. The larger the organization, the greater the opportunity for career progression. Career development is also enhanced by a changing, expanding organization which, over time, needs more employees in positions of responsibility to accommodate its growth.

Career planning is primarily the responsibility of the individual employee; however, organizations need to promote and support career patterns. This requires that individuals be aware of typical career progression patterns within their field, that they be willing to grow and develop within their field, and that they be aware of career opportunities.

Typical career development patterns include several different functions at different levels. The primary purpose of a career development program is to provide a succession of qualified personnel to assume technical and leadership positions within the company.

First, a career development program begins with clear career paths: a series of successive positions in an organization in which success and appropriate development in one position leads to being promoted.

STAFFING A SMALL BUSINESS

Second, the progression should be related to the career field either by function (e.g. marketing, finance, operations) or by industry (e.g., retail clothing, insurance, banking). The progression should also be clearly identified by specific requirements of education and experience necessary for promotion.

Third, the company should provide career development education programs and opportunities. These may be as elaborate as entire internal training programs, or simply funds for seminars, conferences, and workshops, or loans for college or university programs leading to a degree.

In addition, career progression programs require specific actions on the part of the company personnel department. Positions selected as part of a career management program must be monitored. Career employees must be observed to evaluate their management potential. From the top to the lowest supervisor, management must constantly appraise these employees to identify latent talents and assets which could have future value to the company.

The career management program must be publicized to make all employees aware of the program and to enable them to make their desire to participate known to management. Aspirants are identified and counseled regarding what they must do to remain an active candidate for training, development, and promotion consideration. They must also be aware of what assistance the company offers.

The company must guide these individuals in light of their present functioning and performance and also be able to predict their ability to perform in higher positions. Strengths must be clearly documented as well as limitations. The strengths are to be maximized and the appropriate opportunities (training or assignments) offered to reduce the limitations.

The company should be concerned not only with present job assignments and compensatory practices of the organization, but also with future vacancies that must be available to retain promotable employees. Training and developing personnel for positions that do not exist is an invitation for them to seek opportunities elsewhere.

Every business has a career ceiling: some have it high enough that top jobs are occupied by people reaching the end of their personal career patterns. Other companies have ceilings reached well before the end of an individual's career pattern. Employees must either halt their career growth prior to reaching their full potential or go elsewhere to develop further.

Not every organization can or should provide a full, complete career management program for all employees. It is imperative though, that both management and employees be fully aware of the career opportunities and limitations available within the company. A clear understanding on the part of both parties tends to eliminate unpleasant surprises. Some businesses are large enough to provide lifelong career opportunities; some train employees for careers elsewhere. But all organizations must recognize the extent of their career opportunities and manage the employees accordingly.

Chapter 11
Employee Personnel File

Summary of Chapter

Information on personnel and human resource management overflows in detail on what personnel management is. Theories, research results, and current concepts are often described minutely. What is lacking, though, is useful suggestions on developing and maintaining a personnel file. A review of several recent texts reveals that not one has a chapter or section on how to develop and maintain a personnel file.

This chapter is a step-by-step, how-to-do-it guide detailing the purpose of a personnel file, what needs to be in it, how often it should be revised, and how to maintain it. The information presented is based on the authors' practical experience in records management and personnel documentation.

Purpose of Personnel Records

A personnel record is a file where an individual employee's company-related personal information is maintained. It becomes an information system created by the documents that are placed in the file.

Personnel records are, first, a method of maintaining the paperwork on employees. These files serve as a repository for all company data on employees. The data are used to control pay and benefit obligations; develop a record of performance behaviors over time (promotions, pay raises, schooling, termination, etc.) to be used for personnel management; and to file other assorted data on the employee that might affect career decisions.

Examples of the latter may be the collection of information on outside interests or endeavors of the employee. Activities such as volunteer service, civic participation, community involvement, part-time teaching, writing, or local politics, while not directly related to the company, can have an impact on the image of the business.

The second function of a personnel file is to document the basis for personnel decisions. Records can provide a factual picture of what has occurred, when it happened, and, if pertinent, why. Decisions based on accumulated information tend to yield better results, benefiting both the company and the employee.

If a personnel decision is challenged, the employee records may serve to support the reasoning that went into the decision. If a disgruntled employee seeks retribution in court, the results may depend entirely on the documentation the company can provide to support its actions. Many verdicts favor the employee because the business is unable to document the basis for its decision.

STAFFING A SMALL BUSINESS

The contents of a personnel file can be divided into three categories: (1) background information on the employee, (2) pay and benefits records, and (3) performance appraisal records.

Background Information

This section begins with the job application of the employee, along with all paperwork and associated application forms (high school or college transcripts, vocational or trade school records, certifications, letters of recommendation, health records, etc.). This is followed by the interview and selection findings, and the results of any pre-employment testing. Upon being hired, the initial employment records are completed and added to this portion of the file. Included in the file is a copy of the job description for the position being filled.

The employment records can contain very brief forms such as the employee's history record within the organization and a career skills inventory (see Charts 11-1 and 11-2). Some employers may want more detailed forms of employment history which contain personal information, employment data, career skills, education, absentee record, and payroll information (see Chart 11-3). All forms that are put in the personnel records should be constantly updated.

Pay and Benefits Records

The efficient operation of a company-wide total compensation system requires adequate pay and benefit records. Two types of records are maintained.

The first are the company records such as personnel information and payroll authorization form (Chart 11-4) a change of status form (Chart 11-5) monthly and annual attendance records (Charts 11-6 and 11-7) the employee's report of absence (Chart 11-8) and the request to make overtime assignments (Chart 11-9).

The second type of pay and benefit records is federal and state withholding forms. This book covers only the federal forms as each state has its own requirements and forms. For more information on state forms contact the State Comptroller's Office or the Office of the State Treasurer.

The IRS forms begin with the employee completing the IRS Form W-4, Employee Withholding Allowance Certificate. The W-4 is used to collect the exemption information from the new employee on or before the day he or she begins work. The document remains effective until replaced by a new one, which can be turned in by an employee at any time.

The amount to be withheld is calculated on gross wages (before any other deductions) as determined by IRS Circular E, Employer's Tax Guide.

Social Security withholding (Federal Insurance Contributions Act—FICA) is also calculated from Circular E.

EMPLOYEE PERSONNEL FILE

Chart 11-1 Employment History Record

Name   *Robert L. Wilson*

Date of Employment   *May 5, 1980*

Department	Position	Salary Grade	Salary	Action Code	Effective Date
Service	Service Repair	3-3	$1000/mo	H	05-05-80
Service	Service Repair	3-4	$1050/mo	M	05-05-81
Service	Asst. Manager	4-1	$1300/mo	P	07-07-82
Sales	Asst. Manager	4-3	$1400/mo	TR	04-06-83
Service	Manager	6-1	$1680/mo	TR	09-10-84

Action Code:
- H - hire
- RH - rehire
- L - placed on leave
- RL - return from leave
- M - merit increase
- S - shift change
- P - promotion
- TR - transfer
- T - termination
- R - retirement
- O - other

STAFFING A SMALL BUSINESS

Chart 11-2 Employee Career Skills Inventory

Name: Robert L. Wilson   Date: 5-5-80

Position: Service Repair   Department: Service

Major area(s) of educational study:

   AA degree - Business Administration, Maintown Junior College, 1978.

Major area(s) of technical study:

   Small Appliance Repair Course, State Technical Institute, 1979.

Additional training (may include evening classes attended or special training courses):

   8-week course, Service Repair Course, Smallwood Products, 1980.
   4-week course, Service Repair Manager's Course, Smallwood Products, 1982.

Work experience (types of work you have done that are applicable to the work performed for our company; it is not necessary to give specific job):

   May 1979-May 1980, small appliance repair person, Acme's Appliance Sales and Service.

Professional and civic activities:

   Member - Lion's Club
   Member - Westside Athletic Club
   Coach - Westside Little League Team

Hobbies and interests:

   Jogging, baseball, softball

Miscellaneous (other information you would like to have in your file; this may include foreign language competency, awards, etc.):

   1983 - As assistant manager of sales department, helped department win Regional Smallwood Products Best Sales Award (4 day, all expense paid trip to Hawaii).

EMPLOYEE PERSONNEL FILE

Chart 11-3 Employment History Record

PERSONAL INFORMATION

Name: <u>Wilson</u> <u>Robert</u> <u>L.</u>
        last   first   middle

Address: <u>23 Walnut Run</u>
       number and street   apartment

       <u>Canyon</u>   <u>TX</u>   <u>79015</u>
       city   state   zip

Telephone number: <u>806-555-1221</u>

Emergency contact: Jayne Wilson   wife
                    name   relationship

   <u>555-1010</u>   <u>McClaine's Insurance, Canyon</u>
   telephone   address

Date of birth: <u>5-5-58</u>   Sex: <u>X</u> Male   ___Female

Marital status: Single <u>X</u> Married ___ Separated
               ___ Divorced ___ Widowed

Date of last change
of marital status: <u>4-9-80</u>   Number of dependents: <u>2</u>

Exempt - Wage <u>X</u> No   Section
and Hour Law: ___ Yes Date _____ of law: _____

Retirement plan - date enrolled: <u>Atlas Group   5-5-80</u>

Group Insurance Plan No.: <u>0000</u>   Date enrolled: <u>5-5-80</u>

Withholding exemptions: Federal <u>3</u>   State <u>N/A</u>

Union status: N/A

11 - 5

STAFFING A SMALL BUSINESS

EMPLOYMENT INFORMATION

Date of Hire: 5-5-80

Date of Termination:

Reason Terminated:

EMPLOYEE CAREER SKILLS

Degree in Business Administration, Maintown Junior College, 1978

Small Appliance Repair Course, State Technical Institute, 1979

1 year experience as small appliance repair person

EDUCATION

Date	School	Course/Major/Degree
6-76	Canyon High School	Diploma
6-78	Maintown Jr. College	Business - AA Degree
6-79	State Technical Institute	Small Appliance Repair - certificate
9-80	Smallwood Products	Service Repair Course - certificate
6-82	Smallwood Products	Service Repairs Managers Course - certificate

EMPLOYMENT HISTORY

Dates From	To	Department	Position
5-5-80	7-6-82	Service	Service Repair
7-7-82	4-5-83	Service	Assistant Manager
4-6-83	9-9-84	Sales	Assistant Manager
9-10-84		Service	Manager

EMPLOYEE PERSONNEL FILE

ABSENTEE RECORD

Year	Days missed	Reason (use number code)
1980	4	1
1981	none	---
1982	10	5
1983	5	1
1984	none	---

Number code:
1 - Illness/injury
2 - Family problems
3 - Excused with pay
4 - Excused without pay
5 - Jury duty
6 - Military duty
7 - Maternity leave
8 - Weather
9 - Other

SALARY INFORMATION

Effective dates From	To	Hour/Week/Month/Annual Salary	Annual Position/Classification
5-5-80	5-5-81	$1000.00 month	Service Repair 3-3
5-6-81	7-6-82	1050.00 month	Service Repair 3-4
7-7-82	4-5-83	1300.00 month	Asst Manager 4-1
4-6-83	9-9-84	1400.00 month	Asst Manager 4-3
9-10-84		1680.00 month	Manager 6-1

OTHER INFORMATION

STAFFING A SMALL BUSINESS

Chart 11-4 Personnel Information and Payroll Authorization Form

Social Security No.: XXX-XX-XXXX   Effective date: 5-5-80

Name: Robert L. Wilson

Address: 23 Walnut Run

          Canyon, TX 79015

Birthdate: 5-5-58   Sex: Male

Marital status: Married   Racial designation: Caucasian

Date of previous hire: N/A

Changes/Corrections:

JOB ASSIGNMENT SECTION

Department: Service   Position: Service Repair

Employee status: _x_ Regular full-time ___ Regular part-time
                   ___ Other

Accounting codes: XXXXX-SVC

Workers' Compensation: XXXXX

Change to: **Effective date:**   4-6-83

Department: Sales   Position: Assistant Manager

Employee status: _x_ Regular full-time ___ Regular part-time
                  ___ Other

Accounting codes: XXXXX-SAL

Workers' Compensation: XXXXXX

Change to: Effective date: 9-10-84

Department: Sales   Position: Manager

Employee status: _X_ Regular full-time ___ Regular part-time
                   ___ Other

Accounting codes: XXXXX-SVC

Workers' Compensation: XXXXX

EMPLOYEE PERSONNEL FILE

SALARY SECTION

Annual salary: $12,000.00

Rate: ___ Hourly ___ Weekly ___ Biweekly _$1000.00_ Monthly

Pay frequency: ___ Weekly ___ Biweekly _x_ Monthly
___ Other _____

Job grade/Salary level: 3-3   Standard work week: 40 hours

Overtime status: ___ Exempt _x_ O/T over basic workweek

___ O/T over 40 hours ___ Special calculations

___ Other _____

Change to:

Date of last salary change: 5-5-80

Reason for change:

Salary increase: _X_ Merit ___ Promotion
___ Other _____

Salary decrease: ___ Demotion ___ Downgrade
___ Other _____

Rate change (hourly only): ___ General increase
___ Progression increase
___ Special agreement/Rate adjustment

Annual Salary: $12,600.00

Rate: _____ Hourly _____ Weekly

_____ Biweekly _$1050.00_ Monthly

Pay frequency: ___ Weekly ___ Biweekly _X_ Monthly

___ Other _____

Job grade/Salary level: 3-4   Standard workweek: 40 hours

Overtime status: ___ Exempt _X_ O/T over basic workweek

___ O/T over 40 hours ___ Special calculations

___ Other _____

STAFFING A SMALL BUSINESS

Change to: _____ Effective date: 9-10-84

Date of last salary change: 4-6-83

Reason for change:

Salary increase: ____ Merit X Promotion ____ Other _____
Salary decrease: ____ Demotion ____ Downgrade ____ Other _____
Rate change (hourly only): _____ General increase
                           _____ Progression increase
                           _____ Special agreement/Rate adjustment

Annual Salary: $20,160.00

Rate: _____ Hourly   _____ Weekly

      _____ Biweekly $1680   Monthly

Pay frequency: ____ Weekly ____ Biweekly X Monthly

               ____ Other _____

Job grade/Salary level: 6-1   Standard workweek: 40 hours

Overtime status: X Exempt _____ O/T over basic workweek

____ O/T over 40 hours ____ Special calculations

____ Other _____

TAX SECTION

Exclude: ____ FICA ____ Federal

Federal: 3 Number of exemptions   Additional withheld

Changes/corrections:

EMPLOYEE PERSONNEL FILE

LEAVE OF ABSENCE AND TERMINATION SECTION

Leave of absence dates: From _____ through _____

Reason:

Pay status:

Comments/changes:

Termination date:

Reason: Voluntary (resigned) ____

      Involuntary: Released ____ Layoff ____

      Other: Retired ____ Deceased ____

Rehire: Yes ____ No ____

Payment (number of days):
  Separation ____ Lieu of notice ____ Vacation ____

REMARKS

Department Manager _____ Date _____

General Manager _____ Date _____

Personnel _____ Date _____

Bookkeeping _____ Date _____

STAFFING A SMALL BUSINESS

Chart 11-5 Change of Status Form

Please enter the following changes(s) as of   9-10-84

Name: Robert L. Wilson   Clock or Payroll Number: XXXX

Social Security Number: XXX-XX-XXXX

From

Job: Assistant Manager   Department: Sales

Shift: Rate: $1400/month

To

Job: Manager   Department: Service

Shift: Rate: $1680/month

Reason for change:

____	Hired	____	Length of service increase
____	Rehired	____	Reevaluation of existing job
_X_	Promotion	____	Resignation
____	Demotion	____	Retirement
____	Transfer	____	Layoff
____	Merit increase	____	Discharge
____	Leave of absence to (date)_____		

Other reason or explanation:

Authorized by: R.R. Jones   Approved by: A.B. King

EMPLOYEE PERSONNEL FILE

Chart 11-6 Monthly Attendance Record

Month: May 1985

Employee: Robert Wilson   Social Security Number: XXX-XX-XXXX

Department: Service   Supervisor: R.R. Jones

Days missed (indicate reason and time off - record a whole day off as 1.0, one-half day off as 0.50, one-fourth day off as 0.25)

Day	Vacation	Illness/Injury	Other and reason	Excused	Not excused
1					
2					
3					
4					
5					
6					
7					
8					
9					
10					
11					
12					
13					
14					
15					
16					
17					
18					
19					
20					
21					
22					
23					
24					
25					
26					
27					
28					
29					
30					
31					
TOTAL	0	0		0	0

Employee's signature: /s/ R.L. Wilson   Date: 31 May 1985

Supervisor's signature: /s/ R.R. Jones   Date: 5-31-85

STAFFING A SMALL BUSINESS

Chart 11-7 Annual Attendance Record

Year: 1984

Employee: Robert Wilson   Social Security Number: XXX-XX-XXXX

Department: Service   Supervisor: R.R. Jones

Time off: Indicate reason using number code and time off - record a whole day off as 1.0, one-half off as 0.5, one fourth day off as 0.25)

Number code:	1 - Illness/injury 2 - Family problems 3 - Excused with pay 4 - Excused without pay	5 - Jury duty 6 - Military duty 7 - Maternity leave	8 - Weather 9 - Vacation 0 - Other H - Holiday

DAY	JAN	FEB	MAR	APR	MAY	JUN	JUL	AUG	SEP	OCT	NOV	DEC
1	H											
2									H			
3												
4							H					
5												
6												1
7												1
8												1
9										H	1	
10												1
11												1
12									9			
13									9			
14									9			
15					9				9			
16						9			9			
17						9						
18						9						
19						9						
20		H										
21												
22											H	
23												
24												
25												H
26												
27												
28					H							
29												
30												
31												
TOTAL					5				5		5	

Employee's signature: /s/ R.L. Wilson   Date: 31 Dec 1984

Supervisor's signature: /s/ R.R. Jones   Date: 12-31-84

EMPLOYEE PERSONNEL FILE

Chart 11-8 Employee's Absence Report

Name: Robert L. Wilson	Date: 4 March 1985
Department: Service	Job title: Manager
Time reported: 8 a.m.	Received by: R.R. Jones
Estimated days absent: 5	Estimated return: 11 March

Reason: severe cold, sore throat, high temperature

Report Record

Absence reported by: Employee ___ Family __x__ Other employee ___

Friend ___ Supervisor ___ Other ___

How: Telephone __X__ In person ___ Other _____

Absence reason: Sick __X__ Injury ___ Family illness ___

Death in family ___ Transportation ___

Other (explain) _____

Tardiness reason: Sick ___ Injury ___ Family illness ___

Death in family ___ Transportation ___

Other (explain) _____

Department manager: /s/ R.R. Jones   Date: 3-4-85

General manager: Date:

Personnel: Date:

Bookkeeping: Date:

STAFFING A SMALL BUSINESS

Chart 11-9 Request for Overtime Approval

Department: Service	Date: 10 June 1985

Request listed employees be authorized
overtime on the following dates: 12-13-14 June

Name	Purpose	Overtime period From	To	Number of hours
Smith, B.	complete	6 pm	8 pm	2
Young, J.	rush work on Davis contract	6 pm	8 pm	2

Department Supervisor: R.L. Wilson

Approved   x   Disapproved _____

/s/ R. R. Jones	6-10-85
Signature of Department Manager	Date

Federal Unemployment Tax Act (FUTA) taxes are a contribution from the company to help finance the unemployment insurance fund.

If any employees are entitled to an earned income credit (EIC) they may have advance payments of the earned income credit added to their wages or salary. This requires the employee to file an IRS Form W-5 (Earned Income Credit Advance Payment Certificate) with the business. The information provided in Circular E is used to determine the amount of money to be added to their pay (which is not subject to payroll taxes).

Employer compensation to an employee must be reported at the end of the calendar year on IRS Form W-2, Wage and Tax Statement. This form has six parts (duplicate copies); the employer retains copy A and the other copies are distributed according to the instructions for Form W-2. Each employee receives the copies needed for federal, state, and local tax returns.

The withholding information is transmitted to the Social Security Administration using IRS Form W-3, Transmittal of Income and Tax Statements.

The IRS requires employers to keep records on employment taxes for at least four years after the due date or the date the taxes were paid (whichever would be later). These records must be available to IRS representatives upon request. The record keeping requirements include documentation of the proper filing of all required taxes and copies of the forms presented to the employees.

The last form in this section is a Statement of Earnings and Deductions. Two versions are presented as Charts 11-10 and 11-11. This form can be used to record all compensation distribution, contributions, and withholding. It is a company-generated account memorandum of earnings and deductions which compliments the federal and state requirements and furnishes the employee with an on-going wage and benefit record. A copy of the statement is retained in the personnel records of each employee and a copy is given to each employee every payday.

Performance Appraisal Records

The last section of an employee's personnel file is a compilation of all data used to maintain a record of his or her performance over time. Included are the normal annual or semi-annual reports and any special performance reports. If an employee is reassigned, promoted, terminated, or voluntarily changes positions, a formal performance appraisal should be completed for the record.

Other documents that support work-related performance should also be included. These might include professional certifications, letters of commendation or appreciation, school reports, or awards earned or won by the employee.

The next chapter will cover in detail those forms and documentation related to performance appraisal.

STAFFING A SMALL BUSINESS

Keeping Personnel Files

Personnel files contain both financial and personal data. These files constitute confidential information between management and the employee. This can be a double bind to small businesses.

Often the size and structure of the company does not necessitate having a personnel section. Most small businesses do not even have a full-time personnel manager or clerk. Frequently, then, keeping personnel records is relegated to the bookkeeping or accounting sections because many federal and state personnel reporting requirements are already handled by that department.

This can present a problem if the personnel records are to remain confidential. Pay and benefit records are primarily financial, while background information on employees and performance appraisal records are strictly personnel information. If the records are divided so the financial records are maintained by one part of the company and the personnel portion is kept by another, they may become too fragmented to be properly maintained.

One way small businesses may resolve this problem is for the accounting department to maintain the pay and benefit records and place a financial summary in the employee's personnel file on a timely basis. The company officer responsible for employment decisions should maintain the personnel files. In this way, confidentiality and consistency can be maintained.

Personnel actions should be based on facts and honest data. Employee records should not contain any negative information which cannot be substantiated. The records of each employee should be available for them to audit.

EMPLOYEE PERSONNEL FILE

Chart 11-10 Statement of Earnings and Deductions

Company Name

Name: Robert L. Wilson   Social Security Number: XXX-XX-XXXX

Pay period: 1-31 May 1985   Gross: $1680.00   Year to date gross: $8400.00

Deductions for this month

Life insurance	Disability	Dental	Bonds	Retirement	Health
$30.00	$8.70	$13.40	-0-	$100.80	$3.72
Federal withholding tax	State withholding tax	FICA	Allotments		Other
$336.00	$82.10	$118.44	$25.00		-0-

Total Deductions: $718.16

Total Net: $961.84

Year-to-date Deductions

Life insurance	Disability	Dental	Bonds	Retirement	Health
$150.00	$43.50	$67.00	-0-	$504.00	$18.60
Federal withholding tax	State withholding tax	FICA	Allotments		Other
$1680.00	$410.50	$592.20	$125.00		-0-

Total Deductions $3590.80

Total Net $4809.20

STAFFING A SMALL BUSINESS

Chart 11-11 Statement of Earnings and Deductions

	Company Name		
Name: Robert L. Wilson	Social Security Number: XXX-XX-XXXX		
Pay period: 1-31 May 1985	Total gross: $1680.00		
Earnings	Deductions	Allotments	Collections
$1680.00	$336.00 (1) 118.44 (2) 30.00 (3) 8.70 (3) 13.40 (3) 3.72 (3) 100.80 (4) 82.10 (5)	$25.00	
TOTALS	$693.16	$25.00	
		TOTAL DEDUCTIONS	$718.16
		NET EARNINGS	$961.84

Key

(1) Federal withholding tax
(2) FICA
(3) Insurance
(4) Retirement
(5) State withholding tax

EMPLOYEE PERSONNEL FILE

Worksheet 11-1 Employment History Record

Name:

Date of Employment:

Department	Position	Salary grade	Salary	Action code	Effective date

Action code:
- H - hire
- RH - rehire
- L - placed on leave
- RL - return from leave
- M - merit increase
- S - shift change
- P - promotion
- TR - transfer
- T - termination
- R - retirement
- O - other

STAFFING A SMALL BUSINESS

Worksheet 11-2 Employee Career Skills Inventory

Name: Date:

Position: Department:

Major area(s) of educational study:

Major area(s) of technical study:

Additional training (may include evening classes attended or special training courses):

Work experience (types of work you have done that are applicable to the work performed for our company; it is not necessary to give specific job):

Professional and civic activities:

Hobbies and interests:

Miscellaneous (other information you would like to have in your file; this may include foreign language competency, awards, etc.):

EMPLOYEE PERSONNEL FILE

Worksheet 11-3 Employment History Record

PERSONAL INFORMATION

Name: _____
          last   first   middle

Address: _____
    Number and street   apartment

    _____
    city   state   Zip

Telephone number: _____

Emergency contact: _____
          name   relationship

    _____
    telephone   address

Date of birth: _____ Sex: ___ Male ____ Female

Marital status: __ Single __ Married __ Separated __ Divorced __ Widowed

Date of last change
of marital status: _____ Number of dependents: _____

Exempt - Wage   __ No   Section
and Hour Law: __ Yes   Date: of law:

Retirement plan - date enrolled: _____

Group Insurance Plan No.: _____ Date enrolled: _____

Withholding exemptions: Federal _____ State _____

Union status: _____

EMPLOYMENT INFORMATION

Date of hire: _____

Date of termination: _____

Reason terminated: _____

11 - 23

STAFFING A SMALL BUSINESS

EMPLOYEE CAREER SKILLS

EDUCATION

Date	School	Course/Major/Degree

EMPLOYMENT HISTORY

Dates From	To	Department	Position

EMPLOYEE PERSONNEL FILE

ABSENTEE RECORD

Year	Days missed	Reason (use number code)

Number code: 1 - Illness/injury   6 - Military duty
              2 - Family problems   7 - Maternity leave
              3 - Excused with pay   8 - Weather
              4 - Excused without pay 9 - Other
              5 - Jury duty

SALARY INFORMATION

Effective dates		Salary	Hour/Week/Month/Annual	Position/Classification
From	To			

OTHER INFORMATION

STAFFING A SMALL BUSINESS

Worksheet 11-4 Personnel Information and Payroll Authorization Form

Social Security No.:   Effective date:

Name:

Address:

Birthdate: Sex:

Marital status: Racial designation:

Date of previous hire:

Changes/Corrections:

JOB ASSIGNMENT SECTION

Department: Position:

Employee status: __ Regular full-time __ Regular part-time

                 __ Other

Accounting codes:

Workers' Compensation:

Change to: Effective date:

Department: Position:

Employee status: __ Regular full-time __ Regular part-time

                 __ Other

Accounting codes:

Workers' Compensation:

Change to: Effective date:

Department: Position:

Employee status: __ Regular full-time __ Regular part-time

                 __ Other

Accounting codes:

Workers' Compensation:

EMPLOYEE PERSONNEL FILE

SALARY SECTION

Annual salary

   Rate: __ Hourly __ Weekly __ Biweekly __ Monthly

Pay frequency: __ Weekly __ Biweekly __ Monthly __ Other _____

Job grade/Salary level: Standard work week: hours

Overtime status: ___ Exempt ___ O/T over basic workweek
    ___ O/T over 40 hours ___ Special calculations ____ Other_____

Change to

Date of last salary change:

Reason for change:

  Salary increase: ___ Merit ___ Promotion ___ Other _____

  Salary decrease: ___ Demotion ___ Downgrade ___ Other _____

  Rate change (hourly only): ___ General increase

                               ___ Progression increase

                               ___ Special agreement/Rate adjustment

Annual salary

   Rate: __ Hourly __ Weekly __ Biweekly __ Monthly

Pay frequency: __ Weekly __ Biweekly __ Monthly __ Other _____

Job grade/Salary level: Standard work week: hours

Overtime status: ___ Exempt ___ O/T over basic workweek
    ___ O/T over 40 hours ___ Special calculations ____ Other_____

STAFFING A SMALL BUSINESS

Change to: Effective date:

Date of last salary change:

Reason for change:

    Salary increase: ___ Merit ___ Promotion ___ Other _____

    Salary decrease: ___ Demotion ___ Downgrade ___ Other _____

    Rate change (hourly only):   ___ General increase

                                    ___ Progression increase

                                    ___ Special agreement/Rate adjustment

Annual salary

    Rate: __ Hourly __ Weekly __ Biweekly __ Monthly

    Pay frequency: __ Weekly __ Biweekly __ Monthly __ Other _____

    Job grade/Salary level: Standard work week: hours

    Overtime status: ___ Exempt ___ O/T over basic workweek

    ___ O/T over 40 hours ___ Special calculations ___ Other_____

TAX SECTION

Exclude: ___ FICA ___ Federal

Federal: ___ Number of exemptions ___ Additional withheld

Changes/corrections:

EMPLOYEE PERSONNEL FILE

LEAVE OF ABSENCE AND TERMINATION SECTION

Leave of absence dates: From _____ through _____

Reason:

Pay status:

Comments/changes:

Termination date:

Reason: Voluntary (resigned) ____
       Involuntary: Released ____ Layoff ____
       Other: Retired ____ Deceased ____

Rehire: Yes ____ No ____

Payment (number of days):
  Separation ____ Lieu of notice ____ Vacation ____

REMARKS

Department Manager   Date

General Manager   Date

Personnel   Date

Bookkeeping   Date

STAFFING A SMALL BUSINESS

Worksheet 11-5 Change of Status Form

Please enter the following changes(s) as of

Name: Clock or Payroll number:

                                   Social Security number:

From

Job: Department:

Shift: Rate:

To

Job: Department:

Shift: Rate:

Reason for change:

    ____ Hired   ____ Length of service increase

    ____ Rehired   ____ Reevaluation of existing job

    ____ Promotion   ____ Resignation

    ____ Demotion   ____ Retirement

    ____ Transfer   ____ Layoff

    ____ Merit increase   ____ Discharge

    ____ Leave of absence to (date)

Other reason or explanation:

Authorized by: Approved by:

EMPLOYEE PERSONNEL FILE

Worksheet 11-6 Monthly Attendance Record

Month:

Employee: Social Security Number:

Department: Supervisor:

Days missed (indicate reason and time off - record a whole day off as 1.0, one-half day off as 0.50, one-fourth day off as 0.25)

Day	Vacation	Illness/Injury	Other and reason	Excused	Not excused
1					
2					
3					
4					
5					
6					
7					
8					
9					
10					
11					
12					
13					
14					
15					
16					
17					
18					
19					
20					
21					
22					
23					
24					
25					
26					
27					
28					
29					
30					
31					
TOTAL					

Employee's signature: Date:

Supervisor's signature: Date:

STAFFING A SMALL BUSINESS

Worksheet 11-7 Annual Attendance Record

Year:

Employee: Social Security Number:

Department: Supervisor:

Time off: Indicate reason using number code and time off - record a whole day off as 1.0, one-half off as 0.5, one fourth day off as 0.25)

Number code:	1 - Illness/injury	5 - Jury duty	8 - Weather
	2 - Family problems	6 - Military duty	9 - Vacation
	3 - Excused with pay	7 - Maternity leave	0 - Other
	4 - Excused without pay		H - Holiday

DAY	JAN	FEB	MAR	APR	MAY	JUN	JUL	AUG	SEP	OCT	NOV	DEC
1												
2												
3												
4												
5												
6												
7												
8												
9												
10												
11												
12												
13												
14												
15												
16												
17												
18												
19												
20												
21												
22												
23												
24												
25												
26												
27												
28												
29												
30												
31												
TOTAL												

Employee's signature: Date:

Supervisor's signature: Date:

EMPLOYEE PERSONNEL FILE

Worksheet 11-8 Employee Absence Report

Name: _____ Date: _____

Department: _____ Job title: _____

Time reported: _____ Received by: _____

Estimated days absent: _____ Estimated return: _____

Reason: _____

Report Record

Absence reported by: Employee ____ Family ____ Other employee ____

Friend ____ Supervisor ____ Other ____

How: Telephone ____ In person ____ Other _____

Absence reason: Sick ____ Injury ____ Family illness ____

Death in family ____ Transportation ____

Other (explain) _____

Tardiness reason: Sick ____ Injury ____ Family illness ____

Death in family ____ Transportation ____

Other (explain) _____

Department manager: _____ Date: _____

General manager: _____ Date: _____

Personnel: _____ Date: _____

Bookkeeping: _____ Date: _____

STAFFING A SMALL BUSINESS

Worksheet 11-9 Request for Overtime Approval

Department: Date:

Request listed employees be authorized
overtime on the following dates:

Name	Purpose	Overtime period From To	Number of hours

Department Supervisor:

         Approved ___   Disapproved ___

    Signature of Department Manager   Date

EMPLOYEE PERSONNEL FILE

Worksheet 11-10 Statement of Earnings and Deductions

Company Name

Name: Social Security Number:

Pay period: Gross: Year to date gross:

Deductions for this month

| Life insurance | Disability | Dental | Bonds | Retirement | Health |

| Federal withholding tax | State withholding tax | FICA | Allotments | Other |

Total Deductions:

Total Net:

Year-to-date Deductions

| Life insurance | Disability | Dental | Bonds | Retirement | Health |

| Federal withholding tax | State withholding tax | FICA | Allotments | Other |

Total Deductions

Total Net

STAFFING A SMALL BUSINESS

Worksheet 11-11 Statement of Earnings and Deductions

Company Name

Name: Social Security Number:

Pay period: Total gross:

	Earnings	Deductions	Allotments	Collections

TOTALS

TOTAL DEDUCTIONS

NET EARNINGS

Key

    (1) Federal withholding tax
    (2) FICA
    (3) Insurance
    (4) Retirement
    (5) State withholding tax

Chapter 12
Performance Appraisal

Summary of Chapter

Performance appraisal is a method to document work performance over a period of time. At the end of a specified length of time an evaluation or rating is prepared by a supervisor or manager on an employee's ability to accomplish his or her job functions.

A company can simplify and unify its personnel decisions by using a performance appraisal system as an ongoing method for reviewing employee activities. It can be useful in decisions on wage increases, retention in present position, transferring, promoting, demoting, separating, or terminating employees.

An effective appraisal system allows personnel decision makers to distinguish high performers from average or low performers. It can also provide the information needed to predict future performance and ability to handle positions of greater responsibility.

Introduction

Employees are depended on to be attentive to the way they perform their job, to be cooperative with other employees, and to develop constructive attitudes about their work, their department, and their company. To judge how well employees meet their obligations to the company, evaluations must be made. For this reason a performance appraisal system should be used.

Performance appraisals can be a systematic way to track how well employees do their assigned jobs. Strengths and limitations are identified, and job-related areas that need improvement are noted.

Performance appraisals may be used to rank several employees that work in similar positions; to bring consistency to salary decisions; to serve as a document for providing feedback to each employee; to become a historical file covering an employee's tenure with a company; and lastly, to serve as a record against potential legal action from a disgruntled employee.

The performance of all employees should be reviewed annually during the anniversary month of employment. This should be a formal process with a written form being completed. New employees should be reviewed prior to the end of their probationary period. Performance appraisal should be a dual activity, both supervisor and employee work together to evaluate the performance of the employee.

A system may be established using the following procedure. The immediate supervisor or manager completes the performance appraisal form and then discusses it with the employee. The employee is asked to sign the form. The supervisor or manager then makes any salary recommendations. The company bases salary decisions upon overall performance ratings, the absentee record, the manager's recommendation, and the position in salary range.

Probably the most crucial part of the assessment process is the interview with the employee in which the appraisal is discussed. If handled well, the interview can lead to a better understanding between the employee and the supervisor. If any problems are identified, the employee has the opportunity to know just where and how to improve performance. If the interview is not conducted properly, the value of the appraisal is diminished considerably.

After the interview, the evaluation form becomes a part of the employee's personnel file. These evaluations become the strongest determinants of the employee's future with the company.

Types of Evaluations

All evaluations must be based on performance characteristics and behaviors deemed necessary for job success. In the 1960s, experts felt that employee evaluations that were never seen by the workers provided a more accurate estimate of performance. Studies had shown that supervisors who knew their workers would not see the ratings did not rate as high as those who knew their workers would see them.

While this is still true in the 1980s, additional research reveals that employees who know exactly how they stand in the eyes of their supervisors tend to be more satisfied and better able to improve their weaknesses. The practice now is to use the rating forms to provide feedback to the employees on their job performance.

A written appraisal is the most permanent way to document employee performance. It can be done several ways, the differences consisting primarily of the rating format used.

One method is a pure narrative (essay) description of what the employee did. A second method is a pure numerical rating scale where several job characteristics or traits are listed and the evaluator rates performance in each area from low to high. Most rating scales have from three to five different rating measurements. Most organizations use a combination: a numerical index of listed job characteristics and a short narrative summary of the employee's performance.

A serious concern is who should do the rating. The immediate supervisor should be primarily responsible for seeing that the form is properly completed. To offset possible bias in a single evaluator, there are other techniques which can make the evaluation process much more accurate.

STAFFING A SMALL BUSINESS

Examples of ratings are:

    E = Exceeds job requirements
    M = Meets job requirements
    N = Needs some improvement
    U = Unsatisfactory

or

    O = Outstanding
  AA = Above average
    A = Average
    F = Fair
    U = Unsatisfactory

Examples of areas being rated are:

    Attendance
    Ability to handle job
    Ability to get along with others
    Carrying out instructions
    Quality of work
    Quantity of work
    Response to supervision

or

    Quality of work
    Quantity of work
    Dependability
    Cooperation
    Versatility
    Planning
    Initiative
    Leadership

The characteristics or traits used must be related to the job position. This is why the charts in this chapter do not all use the same set of rating characteristics. Each company must draw up its own set.

The evaluation report should be simple, clear, easy to complete, easy to understand, and a fair evaluation of the person in the position. The method used should rely on behaviorally oriented ratings that are objectively derived and have clearly defined standards.

Behaviorally oriented ratings define or describe behaviors that are readily recognized and understood by both employee and supervisor. "Does good work" is not an adequate behavioral description; better to state that the quality of work performed met or exceeded required specifications, was neat, minimized waste of materials, and required minimal supervision. Such behavioral descriptions more clearly define "good work."

PERFORMANCE APPRAISAL

Objectively derived ratings mean that anyone observing the performance or behavior would arrive at the same conclusions regarding the way the work was performed.

If dependability were defined as always arriving at work on time, being ready to start work at the appointed time, completing all assigned work on schedule, turning in reports as required when required, always being ready to help others or always following instruction correctly, then anyone rating a person's performance in this category should have a clear concept of the quality of their dependability. The perception of the ratings should not be subject to a supervisor's personal biases.

Performance appraisal forms should be general enough to cover all areas within an organization yet specific enough to be a meaningful management tool and personnel document. The contents of the form and the method used must be legal; that is, they must represent a valid means of evaluating employee performance without prejudice, discrimination, or bias.

The form must be simple and easy to use. The more responsible and complex the position, the longer the form; for most small businesses, though, a one- or two-page form should suffice. Chart 12-1 is a detailed performance appraisal form with sections to be completed by the evaluator, employee, and the reviewer.

Whatever form is used, the company should ensure that the employee signs it indicating that the performance appraisal has been reviewed and understood.

When to Evaluate

The first few weeks or months serve as the employees' probationary period, when they are evaluated often. Typically the probationary period is for ninety days. During this period the supervisor evaluates the employee's performance and discusses with the employee how he or she is progressing. A suggested schedule for review is at the end of the second week, at the end of the first thirty days, after sixty days, and at the end of the probationary period. Written evaluations are prepared.

Consider not only how the employee is performing but also if it is in the best interests of the company to continue the association. For example, a new employee may be quite capable of performing the job but does not arrive for work on time. If there is not a valid reason for this unacceptable behavior, it may be best to terminate the employee rather than hope the attendance improves.

An employee may be discharged at any time during the probationary period if he or she is not progressing satisfactorily. On the ninety-first day of employment the employee should be classified as permanent full-time and eligible for all benefits, which are dated back to the initial day of employment.

STAFFING A SMALL BUSINESS

Chart 12-1 Performance Appraisal Form

Employee's Name: Ann Webster
Department: Administrative Services   Job: Secretary-Receptionist

Part 1. To be completed by supervisor.

A. Select the block which best describes the employee's level of performance since the last performance appraisal.
E = Exceeds job requirements.
M = Meets job requirements.
N = Needs improvement, meets most but not all job requirements.
U = Unsatisfactory, fails to meet most job requirements.

	E	M	N	U
1. Quality of work: Accuracy, neatness, thoroughness of work. Economy of time and materials. Care of equipment used. Following checklists.	X			
2. Quantity of work: Productive output. Speed and consistency of output.	X			
3. Dependability: Follows instructions. Exercises good judgment, punctuality, attendance, and safety habits.	X			
4. Cooperation: Extent to which employee cooperated with other employees, management and surrounding businesses.	X			
5. Versatility: Resourceful in handling assignment and solving problems. Versatile in application of knowledge and skills.		X		
6. Planning: Ability to plan for immediate and long-range assignments. Sets realistic goals and timetables.		X		
7. Initiative: Diligent work habits. Strong sense of responsibility.		X		
8. Leadership: Inspires confidence, productivity and teamwork. Fair and consistent use of discipline.		X		
9. Salesmanship: Describe and promote products to customers.				
10. Write-in factors: Use any factor not listed that may apply ___seeks___ self-improvement	X			

Overall performance. (Check appropriate box.)
_____   Excellent: Exceeds all job requirements
__x__   Above average: Exceeds most job requirements
_____   Average: Meets all job requirements
_____   Below average: Does not meet all job requirements
_____   Unsatisfactory: Fails to meet most job requirements.

C. How long have you supervised this employee?   1 year

PERFORMANCE APPRAISAL

Supervisor's Comments: Ms. Webster is a valuable employee who does very good work. She is going to college at night studying general business. This will increase her versatility and initiative as she becomes more confident.

Date   1 July 1987   Manager   /s/ Sarah James

Part 2. To be completed by employee.

Please describe what skills or training you have obtained since your last evaluation which will help you in performing your job.

> I am in my second semester at Bradford Community College working toward an AA Degree in secretarial studies.

On this date the Performance Appraisal Form has been discussed with me by my supervisor.

Comments on performance evaluation:

> None

Date   1 July 1987   Employee   /s/ Ann Webster

Part 3. To be completed by general manager.

A. How long have you known this employee? _____1 year_____
B. Current overall performance:

> In the past year Ann has become an above average worker and should continue to improve over time.

3 July 1987   /s/ Dan Stone
Date   Signature of General Manager

STAFFING A SMALL BUSINESS

Chart 12-2 is an example of a new employee probationary performance appraisal form.

Regular employees are usually rated annually. The bookkeeping or personnel department should be responsible for notifying supervisors when performance appraisals are due. Chart 12-3 is an example of a cover letter used to notify managers of what needs to be done. Performance appraisals should also be completed if the rater leaves and more than six months have passed since the last appraisal.

Problems with Performance Appraisal Systems

Even the best designed performance appraisal systems have inherent problems that must be recognized and understood. Probably the most common is rater bias. All managers and supervisors have their own concepts of how to interpret any rating criteria. These may be perceived differently by both the employees being rated and the managers who will make personnel decisions based on the ratings. Having two raters, the employee's supervisor and another manager, tends to even out a strong personal bias.

Another problem area is the use of rating standards that are not equally clear to all users of the system. This misunderstanding may cause different managers to reach different conclusions regarding similar performance. For example, one supervisor may interpret punctual attendance as being at the work station at 8 a.m. while another supervisor takes it to mean arriving in the building at 8 a.m.

Top management can create pressure to inflate or deflate evaluations. A vice president of sales may tell the district sales manager that an outstanding performance rating can only be given to those salespeople who exceed their quotas considerably, regardless of the district's ability to increase sales. A deserving salesperson may not receive a valid rating because his or her district manager was more concerned with pleasing the sales vice president than basing the evaluation on actual performance.

Extraordinary incidents and the proximity of the rating date can have an unjust effect on performance evaluations. A worker who saves the life of a heart-ttack victim may still do poor work yet be rated highly—at least for awhile. An average worker who turns in a superior performance the last few weeks before the rating is due may be rated higher than the total year's performance would suggest, or an outstanding performer who has a poor period just before ratings are due may receive a lower than deserved score.

The last problem area to be recognized is the halo effect. Sometimes certain things tend to over-influence a rater's perception of an employee. A gracious, well-groomed, articulate person may come across as bright, determined, and hard-working when in fact his or her actual performance is average. The personal aura overwhelms the real abilities. Conversely, an outstanding performer with a dowdy appearance and poor interpersonal skills may come across personally as shy and uninteresting and may receive lower than deserved ratings.

PERFORMANCE APPRAISAL

Chart 12-2 New Employee Progress Report

Name: Ralph Edson   Job: Stocking Clerk

Department: Warehouse   Date Employed: 28 June 1987

Check which report this is:

Report I - 2 weeks _____   Report III - 60 days _____
Report II - 30 days   x   Report IV - 90 days _____

	Excellent	Above Average	Average	Below Average	Unsatisfactory
1. Ability to handle job			X		
2. Grooming and neatness			X		
3. Application to work			X		
4. Attendance		X			
5. Response to training			X		
6. Observance of rules			X		
7. Punctuality		X			
8. Carrying out instructions			X		

9. Comments: Ralph is progressing at an average pace. He is always early to work and is one of the last to leave. He appears to be motivated and eager to learn.

10. Recommendations: To continue employment _____yes_____

    To be terminated effective _____

Manager   /s/ John Engals   Date   24 July 1987

Employee /s/ Ralph Edson   Date   24 July 1987

STAFFING A SMALL BUSINESS

Chart 12-3 Performance Appraisal Cover Letter

Instructions This form is to be completed by the department manager and forwarded to the general manager.

When Required

Annual Review - Employee performance is evaluated on an annual basis in the anniversary month.

New Employees - Review each new employee prior to the completion of his or her probationary period.

Termination - Document all terminations by completing this form.

Other - As deemed necessary by management to cover substandard performance, to recognize meritorious performance, or for special purposes such as consideration for educational programs.

How to Prepare

Indicate the level of performance for each characteristics by checking the appropriate column on the form.

Estimate of employee's overall current performance—check the appropriate box that best describes the employee's overall performance. This section is used to describe the employee's typical performance over the entire evaluation period.

Employee's name: Ann Webster

Department: Administrative Services

Type of Review: Annual

Supervisor: Sarah Jones

Date Due: 31 July 1987

Employee Counseling

Completing the employee performance appraisal forms is really the mid-point of the appraisal system; it actually begins with the manager or supervisor establishing an informal file on each worker. In a small business the personnel file may also be the informal file.

The purpose of the informal file is to collect information to be used to write the appraisal when it is due. It would contain copies of letters of recommendation, congratulations, or other documents which reflect on job performance. Training sessions attended, test scores, college courses taken, community service projects undertaken for the company, and informal leadership positions are other examples of data to include in the file.

The supervisor's informal employee file becomes the data bank for the formal appraisal. If the employee has been a problem in areas of attendance, quality of performance, or personal affairs, for example, then the actions that were taken and the results should be recorded and documented in this file. Such documentation could save a company in court if a disgruntled former employee chose to sue over being terminated.

Managers may use two methods of counseling to provide performance feedback to their workers. The first is informal counseling in which the supervisor or manager takes time, on an informal basis, to tell employees how their performance is perceived. Praise, advice, and helpful comments are appropriate informal remarks.

The second method is formal counseling, which generally occurs at annual performance appraisal time, or when an employee is beginning to have noticeable problems, or when the company is considering the employee for a promotion, transfer, or development program.

The formal counseling session may be conducted like the job applicant interviews described in Chapter 9. The focus of the counseling session should be on the employee's strengths and limitations in the job, reinforcing the positive aspects and recommending ways to improve the weaker aspects.

Managers should be trained in how to conduct counseling sessions. Employees should know what the session is to cover and they should have access to the appraisal format so they will know how they are to be evaluated. Chart 12-4 is an example of a performance interview checklist for managers and supervisors.

Employee counseling is a way to inform employees of management's perception and evaluation of their contributions to the company. The supervisor or manager doing the counseling must ensure that the employees realize that average or better performance is a desired goal and that both company and employees should make as much effort as possible to attain this goal. The supervisor should point out that outstanding performance will be rewarded.

STAFFING A SMALL BUSINESS

Chart 12-4 Checklist for Performance Review Interview
(Using Performance Appraisal Form)

Preparation
o   Determine beforehand what you are going to say in the interview.
o   Decide on your major goal for the interview.
o   Determine what is the most important matter to be considered, and steer the discussion to revolve around that point.

Timing
o   Give the employee advance notice of the time of the interview.
o   Schedule enough time for a meaningful exchange to take place.

Location
o   Arrange for a quiet location.
o   Be sure that you have privacy and try to avoid interruptions.

Conduct of the Interview
o   Begin with a few minutes of casual conversation to help relax the employee.
o   Proceed to discuss all aspects of the job; go over each performance characteristic separately. Although you must point out both strengths and weaknesses, it will probably be more effective to discuss positive aspects of performance first.
o   Try to avoid appraisals that are completely negative.
o   Focus on performance, rather than personality.
o   Be constructive, rather than destructive. If there are weaknesses, point them out but emphasize what can be done to rectify the situation.
o   Welcome any questions or complaints that the employee may have.

Summary
o   Briefly review the important points of the appraisal.
o   Carefully restate the details of any proposed courses of action that you have recommended.
o   At the end of the interview, have the employee sign the form (and add any comments they feel are appropriate).

Follow-Up
o   Periodically check the employee's activities to determine whether or not goals discussed at the interview are being attained.
o   Offer assistance in achieving objectives.

PERFORMANCE APPRAISAL

Employee counseling is also used to express concern for an employee's failure to perform satisfactorily. Common problems management faces involve a lack of motivation or interest in the job resulting in substandard performance, substance abuse (drugs or alcohol), family problems, financial deficits, emotional instability, or difficulty with interpersonal relationships. (See Chapter 13.) It is not suggested that supervisors or managers become experts in handling these problem areas, merely that they have enough training to recognize the behavioral symptoms.

Company management should have realistic policies for effectively dealing with these problems. In most cases treatment is beyond the scope of a business. Management, though, must be familiar with the proper referral sources available to employees: institutions such as Alcoholics Anonymous, local credit counseling agencies, city or county family service agencies, churches, and community mental health centers.

The employer who can recognize serious employee problems and guide the employee to help has a better chance of retaining a good employee than one who ignores the danger signs, hoping the problem behaviors will disappear. Early intervention will usually bring more positive results; looking the other way generally only exacerbates the problem.

Personnel Actions

Upon completion of the performance appraisal and counseling session, decisions must be made. In most cases the decisions are made before the counseling session and the session is used to inform the employee of the decision and its impact on the employee. Sometimes, though, decisions need input from the employee and the counseling session is used to obtain that input.

If the performance appraisal results in a recommendation for a salary increase (see Chart 12-5), then the counseling session may be used primarily to praise the employee and present the reward.

A common use of the counseling session is to develop a plan for upgrading or improving performance. This may be a response to recognized deficiencies in an employee's job performance, or it may be a plan to prepare the employee for transfer or promotion.

Chart 12-6 is an example of an employee performance improvement plan and Chart 12-7 is an example of the follow-up report used to track progress of the plan. In most cases employees appreciate feedback on their performance and will eagerly receive the opportunity to improve their performance.

STAFFING A SMALL BUSINESS

Chart 12-5 Salary Change Recommendation

Name: Carol Rice	Date: 7 August 1987
Job Title: Senior Sales Supervisor	Department: Women's Wear

An increase in pay is recommended for the following reason:

    ___ Probationary (end of first 90 days)

    ___ Merit

    ___ Wage hour

    _x_ Promotion. Indicate new job title if different from above

    ___ Other. Indicate reason

If the salary change is based on merit or promotion, complete this section. Performance assessment form is attached. Yes _x_ No ___

If no, date of last appraisal

Recommendation

Current salary	$_____ hourly	$_____ weekly	$13,500 annually
Recommended increase	$_____ hourly	$_____ weekly	$1,200 annually
New salary	$_____ hourly	$_____ weekly	$14,700 annually

Comments

Department Manager: /s/ Alex Roscoe	Date: 7 August 1987

Approved by:

General Manager: /s/ Janet Goulde	Date: 13 August 1987

Effective date of increase: 1 September 1987

PERFORMANCE APPRAISAL

Chart 12-6 Employee Performance Improvement Plan

Name: Ken Thomas	Date: 29 May 1987
Job title: Mechanic	Department: Service
Date of employment: 26 Jan 87	Date entered position: 26 Jan 87

Date of last performance review: 24 April 1987

Overall performance rating: Average

General Performance Overview

Listed below are performance areas pertinent to continued employment. Please check for each area applicable to this employee's position. Leave blank if the area is not important in fulfillment of position responsibilities.

	Unsatis-factory	Satis-factory	Commend-able
Quantity of work		X	
Quality of work		X	
Dependability		X	
Cooperation	X		
Versatility		X	
Job knowledge	X		
Need for supervision		X	
Follows rules		X	
Attendance		X	
Ability to handle job	X		
Carry out instructions		X	
Attitude	X		

Reason for low performance rating:
Ken is the junior mechanic in the auto service department and the least knowledgeable. He is in his late 30's and finds it very difficult to be supervised by more knowledgeable mechanics who also happen to be 10 to 15 years younger than him. As a result he tends to be brusque and sometimes abusive or offensive, especially when they point out mistakes he has made or is making. Ken is a good worker but he has to learn to relate better to his co-workers and supervisors.

STAFFING A SMALL BUSINESS

Performance Improvement Plan:

1. Explain to other mechanics to be aware of Ken's sensitivity to his age and experience vs. theirs and to use more tact.

2. Make it clear to Ken that he needs to learn to improve and maintain his job skills and he must learn from the younger but more experienced mechanics.

3. Have Ken ask for help when he is not sure of what to do.

4. Manager will give as much attention to Ken as possible. Work with Ken as much as possible as a training supervisor. Provide tech manuals for home study.

Length of time proposed for upgrading performance: 2   weeks.

Review dates: none

Date   29 May 87   Employee   /s/ K. Thomas

Date   29 May 87   Department Manager   /s/ Don Rogers

PERFORMANCE APPRAISAL

Chart 12-7 Follow-Up Report of Employee Performance Improvement Plan

Name: Ken Thomas   Date: 12 June 1987

Job Title: Mechanic   Department: Service

Date improvement plan started: 29 May 1987

Results:

_____ Job performance improved to satisfactory level.

__x__ Job performance improved but still below acceptable standards.

_____ Job performance not improved; plan continued or extended.

_____ Job performance not improved; employee transferred to date.

_____ Job performance not improved; employee discharged.

Narrative Report

Ken has made some progress. The younger mechanics are more tactful in their approach to Ken. Ken is trying hard to recognize that they want him to improve—not belittle him.

Ken is studying technical manuals at home at night and he is becoming a better mechanic and more tolerant of advice from the younger mechanics. Plan to continue for 2 more weeks.

Date: 12 June 1987   Employee: /s/ Ken Thomas

Date: 12 June 1987   Department Manager: /s/ Don Rogers

STAFFING A SMALL BUSINESS

Worksheet 12-1 Performance Appraisal Form

Employee's Name:
Department: Job:

Part 1. To be completed by supervisor.

A. Select the block which best describes the employee's level of performance since the last performance appraisal.
E = Exceeds job requirements.
M = Meets job requirements.
N = Needs improvement, meets most but not all job requirements.
U = Unsatisfactory, fails to meet most job requirements.

	E	M	N	U
1. Quality of work: Accuracy, neatness, thoroughness of work. Economy of time and materials. Care of equipment used. Following checklists.				
2. Quantity of work: Productive output. Speed and consistency of output.				
3. Dependability: Follows instructions. Exercises good judgment, punctuality, attendance, and safety habits.				
4. Cooperation: Extent to which employee cooperated with other employees, management and surrounding businesses.				
5. Versatility: Resourceful in handling assignment and solving problems. Versatile in application of knowledge and skills.				
6. Planning: Ability to plan for immediate and long-range assignments. Sets realistic goals and timetables.				
7. Initiative: Diligent work habits. Strong sense of responsibility.				
8. Leadership: Inspires confidence, productivity and teamwork. Fair and consistent use of discipline.				
9. Salesmanship: Describe and promote products to customers.				
10. Write-in factors: Use any factor not listed that may apply _____				

Overall performance. (Check appropriate box.)
_____ Excellent: Exceeds all job requirements
_____ Above average: Exceeds most job requirements
_____ Average: Meets all job requirements
_____ Below average: Does not meet all job requirements
_____ Unsatisfactory: Fails to meet most job requirements

C. How long have you supervised this employee?

PERFORMANCE APPRAISAL

Supervisor's Comments:

_____
Date   Manager

Part 2. To be completed by employee.

Please describe what skills or training you have obtained since your last evaluation which will help you in performing your job.

_____

On this date the Performance Appraisal Form has been discussed with me by my supervisor.

Comments on performance evaluation:

_____
Date   Employee

Part 3. To be completed by general manager.

A. How long have you known this employee? _____
B. Current overall performance:

_____

_____
Date   Signature of General Manager

STAFFING A SMALL BUSINESS

Worksheet 12-2 Performance Appraisal Cover Letter

Instructions   This form is to be completed by the department manager and forwarded to the general manager.

When Required

Annual Review - Employee performance is evaluated on an annual basis in the anniversary month.

New Employees - Review each new employee prior to the completion of his or her probationary period.

Termination - Document all terminations by completing this form.

Other - As deemed necessary by management to cover substandard performance, to recognize meritorious performance, or for special purposes such as consideration for educational programs.

How to Prepare

Indicate the level of performance for each characteristics by checking the appropriate column on the form.

Estimate of employee's overall current performance—check the appropriate box that best describes the employee's overall performance. This section is used to describe the employee's typical performance over the entire evaluation period.

Employee's name:

Department:

Type of Review:

Supervisor:

Date Due:

PERFORMANCE APPRAISAL

Worksheet 12-3 Salary Change Recommendation

Name: Date:

Job Title: Department:

An increase in pay is recommended for the following reason:

    ___ Probationary (end of first 90 days)

    ___ Merit

    ___ Wage hour

    ___ Promotion. Indicate new job title if different from above

    ___ Other. Indicate reason

If the salary change is based on merit or promotion, complete this section. Performance assessment form is attached. Yes ___   No ___

If no, date of last appraisal

Recommendation

    Current salary $_____ hourly $_____ weekly _____ annually

    Recommended increase $_____ hourly $_____ weekly _____ annually

    New salary $_____ hourly $_____ weekly _____ annually

Comments

Department Manager: Date:

Approved by:

General Manager: Date:

Effective date of increase:

STAFFING A SMALL BUSINESS

Worksheet 12-4 Employee Performance Improvement Plan

Name: Date:

Job title: Department:

Date of employment: Date entered position:

Date of last performance review:

Overall performance rating:

General Performance Overview

Listed below are performance areas pertinent to continued employment. Please check for each area applicable to this employee's position. Leave blank if the area is not important in fulfillment of position responsibilities.

	Unsatis-factory	Satis-factory	Commend-able
Quantity of work			
Quality of work			
Dependability			
Cooperation			
Versatility			
Job knowledge			
Need for supervision			
Follows rules			
Attendance			
Ability to handle job			
Carry out instructions			
Attitude			

Reason for low performance rating:

PERFORMANCE APPRAISAL

Performance Improvement Plan:

1.

2.

3.

4.

Length of time proposed for upgrading performance:

Review dates:

Date   Employee

Date   Department Manager

STAFFING A SMALL BUSINESS

Worksheet 12-5 Follow-Up Report of Employee Performance Improvement Plan

Name: Date:

Job Title: Department:

Date improvement plan started:

Results:

_____ Job performance improved to satisfactory level.

_____ Job performance improved but still below acceptable standards.

_____ Job performance not improved; plan continued or extended.

_____ Job performance not improved; employee transferred to date.

_____ Job performance not improved; employee discharged.

Narrative Report

Date: Employee:

Date: Department Manager:

Chapter 13
Handling Disciplinary Problems

Summary of Chapter

Counseling is one of the most important aspects of handling problem employees. This chapter addresses each step in the process that management may use to effectively intervene and rectify a disciplinary problem or, as may be necessary, to decide to terminate the errant employee. Handling the counseling session properly and documenting the steps in the disciplinary process are the two most important points taken up.

Introduction

There are many ways that disciplinary problems surface. Most often a breach of employment conduct is noted and dealt with on the spot by the immediate supervisor. There are also occasions when on-the-spot corrections are not sufficient and stronger actions must be taken.

Employee counseling can range from simple advice on the job to helping an employee find the community resources available for problems beyond the scope of company management.

Counseling Sessions

The counseling session gives the supervisor the opportunity to engage in a one-to-one interaction with an employee. The purpose is to provide the employee with feedback concerning a behavior problem, rule infraction, or unsatisfactory performance. The session should be used to point out to the employee conduct that is objectionable, explain what is expected instead, provide guidance regarding how the employee can change the unacceptable behavior, and note the consequences of not changing.

Typically a breach of acceptable behavior has reached a point where it can no longer be tolerated. Someone in the supervisory chain realizes that informal warnings are going unheeded. More stringent action is needed. Before deciding what action should be taken, the supervisor must collect as much information as possible.

The counselor must ensure that all the facts are accurate and verified. The counselor should talk to witnesses to understand the circumstances of the situation. When this has been done, the supervisor is ready to discuss the problem with the employee.

The counseling session is best held in a private location. It should not be conducted as an inquisition or a punitive meeting but as one in which a concerned manager is trying, along with the employee, to ascertain why things are not going well.

Only those people involved in the problem behavior should be present. Usually, this includes the employee and a supervisor or manager. In most cases the counseling is the result of an employee's failure to appropriately respond to a supervisor's informal warning. When the informal advice is not heeded, then formal counseling may be in order.

The counselor should inform the employee of the accusations of unacceptable behavior. Cite facts, not impressions. For example, say, "You were 30 minutes late three days last week," not, "I hear you're not coming to work much any more." After explaining the infractions, ask for the employee's explanation. Do not get caught in semantic explanations or cross-accusations. Do not let the employee wander off the subject by arguing or stating that the supervisor is always picking on him or her.

If the employee denies any wrongdoing, point out the facts that belie the employee's version. If the employee brings up situations or events that were unknown, halt the session until they can be checked out.

In almost all instances, if the supervisors are doing their jobs, they will have documentation of the violations (witnesses, time cards, written notices, etc.) and the counselor's job will not be that of refereeing a disagreement but providing guidance and advice.

Sometimes the referral for disciplinary action is the result of managerial decisions that create genuine confusion about what is required of an employee. In order to avoid this, managers should:

o Respect each employee as a person who has a contribution to make to the organization.

o Explain company standards and procedures and their role in the work unit to employees.

o Establish an on-going work system that includes planning, organizing, leading, and controlling.

o Supervise constructively and consistently following the guidelines set forth by management.

Assuming that the above suggestions are being followed and the complaints are valid, the counseling session can continue.

HANDLING DISCIPLINARY PROBLEMS

What to Do

The counselor should remain emotionally aloof and maintain control of the session. If the employee refuses to participate, disavows any wrongdoing or displays an indifferent attitude, merely review the facts and point out the consequences if the unacceptable behavior continues.

If the employee acknowledges the errant behavior then together employee and manager can examine acceptable or desired behaviors, and the best way to achieve them. There may be extenuating circumstances, such as family discord or personal problems that interfered with job duties. If this is the case, referral to an appropriate outside agency or clinic may help alleviate the problem.

Managers must recognize that help or guidance will be more acceptable if the employees feel the disciplinary action was fair and impartial. The consequences must be preceded by sufficient warnings so the disciplined person will not feel singled out or unjustly punished.

The disciplinary action must come soon after the aberrant behavior; long time lags suggest that management is not sure what to do. This perception by other employees does not usually serve to discourage the behavior, and may even reinforce it.

The discipline itself should relate to both the offending behavior, the severity of the circumstances, and the individuals involved. Consistency should be practiced. The consequences should be in line with other disciplinary actions in similar situations.

When it is decided what should be done, the session should be formalized in writing. This creates a permanent document of the counseling session and provides both employee and management with the same record of what occurred.

It may help to have the employee sign a record of the session, which verifies that the counseling session occurred as stated. If a signature is required due to the severity of the offense, it may be helpful to have a witness in the room during the session. This could be the employee's supervisor or the manager's supervisor. If the employee refuses to sign, then the manager and the witness can verify in writing what took place and the employee's refusal to sign.

While counseling may be thought of in terms of problems or discipline, it can also be used to assist employees in developing their potential for advancement. In this case the session is used to review past performance and provide guidance for career progression.

STAFFING A SMALL BUSINESS

Documentation

Fairness and consistency are important elements in enforcing company rules. Written records help ensure that the employee and manager understand the events. This is not to suggest that managers keep diaries on employee behavior. But it is recommended that if disciplinary action is called for, then a written record be made.

Chart 13-1 is an example of an employee warning form; the employee is given a copy with recommended corrective actions. Chart 13-2 is an example of a consultation report concerning misconduct and suggested corrective measures. Chart 13-3 is an example of a suspension notice. These three forms require both the employee and supervisor to sign them.

The last chart (13-4) is an example of a discharge recommendation. This form details the disciplinary history and corrective measures implemented; more than one management signature is required.

Documentation protects the company and the employee. Once a disciplinary action has been satisfactorily resolved, this is also reflected in the employee's records.

HANDLING DISCIPLINARY PROBLEMS

Chart 13-1 Employee Warning

To:	Roger Burns	Date:	12 June 1987
From:	R.L. Wilson	Title:	Supervisor

Subject: Unexcused absence from work

This is a written warning regarding the event described below. Failure to correct the conduct could result in further disciplinary action.

This is the second time this month you have failed to report to work without an acceptable excuse. Continuation of this behavior can result in termination of your employment.

Supervisor: /s/ R.L. Wilson

I hereby acknowledge that I was informed of the misconduct and corrective action described above. I further acknowledge receipt of a copy of this written warning.

Date 12 June 87   Employee /s/ R. Burns

Original: Employee's personnel file
 Copy: Employee
 Copy: Supervisor

STAFFING A SMALL BUSINESS

Chart 13-2 Consultation with Employee

This is to confirm that   <u>R.L. Wilson</u>   Supervisor

Counseled with   <u>Roger Burns</u>   Employee

About   Unexcused absences from work
          Nature of misconduct and corrective action required

This is the third time this month you have failed to show up for work (4, 12 and 17 June). If you have one more unexcused absence in the next six months your employment will be terminated.

The above named employee was informed that failure to correct the conduct described above could result in disciplinary action.

Date	18 June 1987	Supervisor	/s/ R.L. Wilson
Date	18 June 1987	Employee	/s/ R. Burns

Original: Employee's personnel file
   Copy: Employee
   Copy: Supervisor

HANDLING DISCIPLINARY PROBLEMS

Chart 13-3 Suspension Notice

On this <u>8th</u> day of <u>July</u>, 1987 <u>Roger Burns</u> (employee) was notified that <u>he</u>/she was being suspended from work without pay from <u>8 July</u> through <u>19 July</u> and instructed to report to <u>Ms. Kristi Mills</u>, Payroll Clerk at <u>9 a.m.</u> o'clock on <u>8 July</u>

Nature of misconduct: Excessive unexcused absences from work.

Corrective action required: Upon termination of this suspension any further unexcused absence will result in discharge from work.

Date   8 July 1987   Supervisor   /s/ R.L. Wilson

I hereby acknowledge that I was informed of the misconduct and corrective action described above. I further acknowledge receipt of a copy of this notice of suspension.

Date   8 July 1987   Employee   /s/ Roger Burns

Original: Employee's personnel file
  Copy: Employee
  Copy: Supervisor

STAFFING A SMALL BUSINESS

Chart 13-4 Discharge Recommendation

Department: Machine Shop

Name of employee: Roger Burns

Detailed explanation and reasons for discharge:

Unexcused absences on 4 June, 12 June, 17 June, 6 July, and 6-7 August, 1987.

Prior consultation and discipline: Verbal reprimand on 4 June, written warning on 12 June, counseling session on 18 June, and two-week suspension from 8 to 19 July 1987.

Discharge recommendation:

Date 12 Aug 1987	Signature and Title	/s/ R.L. Wilson Supervisor
Date 12 Aug 1987	Signature and Title	/s/ Bill Johnson Machine Shop Foreman

Approvals:

Date 12 Aug 1987	Signature and Title	/s/ Randy Watson Personnel
Date 12 Aug 1987	Signature and Title	/s/ Sandra Anderson Executive VP
Date	Signature and Title	

Effective date of discharge   12 August 1987

HANDLING DISCIPLINARY PROBLEMS

Worksheet 13-1 Employee Warning

To: Date:

From: Title:

Subject:

This is a written warning regarding the event described below. Failure to correct the conduct could result in further disciplinary action.

_____
Supervisor

I hereby acknowledge that I was informed of the misconduct and corrective action described above. I further acknowledge receipt of a copy of this written warning.

_____
Date   Employee

Original: Employee's personnel file
  Copy: Employee
  Copy: Supervisor

STAFFING A SMALL BUSINESS

Worksheet 13-2 Consultation with Employee

This is to confirm that _____ (supervisor)

counseled with _____(employee)

about (nature of misconduct and corrective action required)

The above named employee was informed that failure to correct the conduct described above could result in disciplinary action.

Date   Supervisor

Date   Employee

Original: Employee's personnel file
   Copy: Employee
   Copy: Supervisor

Worksheet 13-3 Suspension Notice

On this _____ day of _____, 19____

_____ (employee) was notified that he/she was being suspended from work without pay from _____ through _____ and instructed to report to _____ at _____ o'clock on _____ .

Nature of misconduct:

Corrective action required:

_____   _____
Date   Supervisor

I hereby acknowledge that I was informed of the misconduct and corrective action described above. I further acknowledge receipt of a copy of this notice of suspension.

_____   _____
Date   Employee

Original: Employee's personnel file
   Copy: Employee
   Copy: Supervisor

STAFFING A SMALL BUSINESS

Worksheet 13-4 Discharge Recommendation

Department:

Name of employee:

Detailed explanation and reasons for discharge:

Prior consultation and discipline:

Discharge recommendation:

Date   Signature and Title

Date   Signature and Title

Approvals:

Date   Signature and Title

Date   Signature and Title

Date   Signature and Title

Effective date of discharge:

Chapter 14
Training and Development

Summary of Chapter

Survival in the competitive climate of the business world often depends on current knowledge. Knowledge regarding the latest operating technologies, product development, management procedures, market trends, and more cost effective ways of running the business is required constantly. This knowledge is most often acquired via some form of training.

Chapter 14 examines the necessity for training in small businesses, what kinds of training are available and the scope of each type, how to determine training needs and select training resources, and how to evaluate a training program. Included at the end of the chapter are a review of legal considerations of company-sponsored training and development programs, and ways to protect the training investment.

Why Is Training Needed?

Employee training is simply one more way for a company to increase the worth of its assets. In many cases employees are a company's most valuable resource and its most expensive investment in terms of cost and time. For employees to remain qualified, ongoing company-sanctioned training should be a part of the operating philosophy.

Training can fulfill the business' current educational needs as well as prepare employees for future technological and professional development. The three-person independent insurance agency that uses correspondence courses and the 150-employee manufacturing plant that has its own training people both recognize the importance of company training. A projection of small business operations in the late 1980s and early 1990s emphasizes the importance of trained employees.

Salaries for lower level positions will continue to increase, making the hiring and training of entry level positions an expensive proposition that will cost more each year. The size of the work force will continue to increase but at a slower pace. Job specialization will become more prevalent than job generalization. Training within a company will be the means to cross-train specialists to accommodate more company functions.

As more businesses acquire computer systems, repetitive, manual office tasks will become automated. Clerical, administrative and secretarial staff will require training on the operations of more complex equipment. The demand is growing for professional managers that possess technical competency within narrow, specific fields. College students now in school can obtain the necessary entry level background training needed, but practicing managers must go back to school or take specialized professional training.

Whether meeting demands of today or tomorrow, it is apparent that company-sponsored training, in-house or external, is a necessary part of operating a business.

Training is conducted to improve skills and to overcome current deficiencies. Managers are sent to seminars that explain the supervisory process; administrative personnel attend workshops and training sessions to upgrade the skills used in their daily work routine; salespeople attend conferences and lectures designed to improve their selling skills and grant them additional product knowledge; skilled workers receive instruction in technical advances of new machinery and products. In these cases, the training is not in anticipation of a future need but to improve current business practices.

Company-sponsored training is also a matter of preparing for a future need. People are trained to obtain the qualification for more job responsibility, in their present positions or a higher one, or both. Most training for future needs is anticipatory, that is, it is planned with certain goals and objectives in mind based on the company's long-term plans.

All employees can benefit from training in areas such as management, technical proficiency, product development, administrative skills, sales techniques, customer relations, or equipment operations whether it is to remain current or to assume future responsibilities. Each business will need to decide which skills, abilities and knowledge it requires to remain marketable and competitive. Training programs, therefore, are designed to meet the needs of today as well as for the future.

Evaluating Training Needs

The recognition of a need for training, in many small businesses, arises out of the decision to expand or implement a new business operation.

Expanding into a different product line, installing new shop equipment, computerizing the bookkeeping department, purchasing computerized cash registers which record sales and inventory levels, adding a new department, or opening up a new branch office all require skills that in many cases are not presently available within a business.

The additional skills must be acquired either by hiring or training. Good planning ensures that these new needs are understood and that provisions are made to acquire the needed skills in a cost effective, timely manner.

Less visible, but no less important, are skill deficiencies which adversely affect the efficiency or productivity of a business. These deficiencies are detected through a training needs evaluation.

A training needs evaluation can examine individual employees, the organization as a whole, or specific functional areas (administration, sales, production). It can also be used to analyze the current state of skill levels within an organization, compare them to known future needs, and predict where future deficiencies will occur. This knowledge can be used to develop training programs to qualify employees for future positions.

Whether the evaluation is aimed at specific people, specific operations, or the organization as a whole, the procedure is the same. A training needs evaluation form is designed and filled out. The form can be completed by the employee's supervisor, by the employee, or by both. Having both complete the form allows management to recognize the employee's perception of his or her strengths and limitations as compared to the supervisor's assessment.

No single form can be used throughout any organization unless everyone does the exact same job. The format may be the same, but the skill areas to be evaluated differ with each position. Charts 14-1 and 14-2 are examples of training needs evaluation forms.

The skill areas to be assessed should come from the job description. If it becomes apparent that skill areas are needed which are not on the job description, then rewriting the job description may become necessary.

An analysis of those areas rated below average or poor (or maybe even average) should help pinpoint the need for employee training. Additional evaluations may be needed to include observing the employee(s); giving specific skill tests such as typing, equipment usage, or product knowledge; or evaluating the output of the employee(s) such as typed correspondence, finished products, customer satisfaction, or sales invoices. These additional evaluation methods should pinpoint what training is needed.

The form may also be used to access the current knowledge and skills of personnel being considered for promotion (see Chart 14-2). It can help identify strengths and weaknesses applicable to their career development.

Types of Training

Employee training can be conducted at the business or off the premises, by company personnel or by outside professionals. Regardless of where it is held or who is in charge of the training, there are several presentation methods.

- o Lecture. This method employs one or more instructors who make a presentation to a group of people. It is a fast and effective way to present information to a group of people, although audience participation is limited. The audience can be virtually any size.

- o Conference or Seminar. This method is similar to the lecture except it involves audience participation. It is more of an exchange of knowledge

STAFFING A SMALL BUSINESS

Chart 14-1 Training Needs Evaluation Form

Employee: Ronald Hanes	Date: 20 August 1987
Position: Senior Sales Clerk	Department: Sporting Goods

Supervisor: Judy Eastman

EX = Excellent
AA = Above Average
A = Average
BA = Below Average
UN = Unsatisfactory

Skill Level

Skill area: Sales	EX	AA	A	BA	UN
Interpersonal skills				X	
Product knowledge				X	
Prepare sales receipt		X			
Handling cash register		X			
Handling credit sales		X			
Selling skills			X		

Supervisor's comments:

Ron's technical skills using the equipment is way above average. He is not as knowledgeable regarding all of the products we sell (he transferred into our department from auto parts as a senior sales clerk). This limited knowledge thus affects his ability to interact with our customers.

Supervisor's recommendations:

Send Ron to our distributor's annual one-week product demonstration course. This should increase his product knowledge and overcome his reluctance to interact with the customers.

Supervisor /s/ Judy Eastman   Date 20 August 1987

TRAINING AND DEVELOPMENT

Chart 14-2 Training Needs Evaluation Form

Employee: Jim Halloman	Date: 24 July 1987
Position: Draftsman	Department: Drafting
Supervisor: Steve Colter	

EX = Excellent
AA = Above Average
 A = Average
BA = Below Average
UN = Unsatisfactory

	Skill Level				
Skill Area: Production	EX	AA	A	BA	UN
Ability to read blueprints	X				
Ability to follow directions	X				
Ability to use equipment	X				
Ability to pace work	X				
Ability to complete work schedule on time	X				
Ability to maintain equipment		X			
Ability to effectively schedule preventive maintenance	- - - - - - - N/A - - - - - - - - -				
Ability to perform quality inspection on completed product	- - - - - - - - N/A - - - - - - - - -				
Ability to forecast raw materials needs	- - - - - - - N/A - - - - - - - - - -				

Supervisor's comments: Jim is doing an excellemt job as a draftsman. I feel he is ready to be promoted to a position in our production department--to do this he needs additional training.

Supervisor's recommendations: Recommended Jim be assigned to our two-week OJT program as a production assistant for training and evaluation for permanent promotion.

Supervisor: /s/ Steve Colter   Date: 25 July 1987

STAFFING A SMALL BUSINESS

than just the presentation of information. Because of the expanded leader-audience participation, it takes longer than a lecture and the audience size should be restricted to maximize audience participation.

o   Audio-Visual Self-Learning. This self-study method easily adapts a training program to individual employee schedules. It is a programmed learning package where an individual uses printed materials such as textbooks, workbooks, or question-and-answer books with audio-visual equipment. The information is presented both orally and in pictures in conjunction with the printed information in the books. This way the student can see, hear, and read the information. Students can learn at their own pace.

   While the individual audio-visual learning packages and viewing equipment can be expensive, when amortized over time or several individuals, the cost becomes relatively low. And, as a permanent part of the company's training system, the learning materials are readily available to employees when needed. Additional learning packages or updates to existing ones may also be acquired.

o   Correspondence. This is the forerunner of audio-visual self-paced learning. The individual receives a study packet containing learning resources such as books, charts, examples, or tests, and begins the program.

   Some companies combine correspondence programs with on-site instruction; supervisors may lecture on different chapters or sections in the workbook. Another version is to have several correspondence students meet together at a specific time for a group discussion on the chapter. This group participation enhances comprehension and reinforces learning.

o   On-the-Job Training (OJT). This method of training often has two levels. One is an informal process of training by assigning a new employee to an experienced employee for a period of time to learn what to do and how to do it.

   The second method, apprenticeship, is a more formal training program with required phases that all have specified time requirements to be spent in each area. Apprentice training is usually a less flexible form of training while in the actual work environment.

   Typically the informal OJT is designed to quickly qualify a person to successfully perform specific job functions. An apprentice program is long and more demanding because it usually qualifies the apprentice for a specific trade rather than just a job function.

The methods of training can be cognitive (primarily reading, writing, listening, and talking); experiential (applying learned concepts in simulated situations); or skill applications (learning on real equipment or in the actual situation). Training programs may use any combination of these methods.

Computer training, for example, uses all three learning components. The cognitive portion involves classroom lectures presenting information on computer systems and how they work. The experiential portion involves working practice problems on a computer, and the skills application is the supervised training received while actually using the company computer in real work situations.

The following is a recommendation outline to use when developing training programs.

o Develop Learning Goals. The entire training program should be based on the acquisition of specific learning concepts, skills, or abilities. The goals should be measurable by some kind of testing procedures (e.g., typing 50 words per minute without mistakes, packing ten cartons of widgets in 30 minutes, grinding and polishing one engine valve every half-hour). The attainment of the stated goals should provide the student with a skill or ability level not previously present.

o Design the Format. The goals to be met usually dictate the type and method of training needed. A program should be designed to take the students from where they are to where they should be. Complexity of the subject and the time available for teaching and studying must be considered. The program should also lend itself to being evaluated by measuring student progress.

o Pre-Testing. Before each employee begins the training, a pre-test should be conducted to measure the skill level before the program begins. This will be compared to a post-test to see how much learning has been assimilated.

o Post-Testing. Conduct the same evaluation as used in the pre-test. Compare differences to determine how much learning took place.

o Follow-Up Evaluation. This may be a repeat of the tests or an informal evaluation of student or supervisor. This is done some time (several weeks to several months) after the training to see how effective the training was as it applied to the actual job environment.

If the business has the qualified personnel, the entire training program may be conducted in-house. If the company lacks personnel, equipment, or facilities, the use of external resources may be necessary.

Chart 14-3 is an example of a training checklist to be used if the program is conducted in-house. Chart 14-4 is an example of a training program evaluation for the trainers to receive immediate feedback on how the students perceived the training. Chart 14-5 shows the format of the report written at the end of the course. Chart 14-6 is a list of sources of information for designing or contracting for training programs.

Making Training Effective

There are several things that can be done to enhance the effectiveness of training programs. The most important concept is that the training must be

STAFFING A SMALL BUSINESS

Chart 14-3 Training Checklist

1. Determine subject to be covered.

2. Determine the group to be trained.

3. Research to determine the need for the subject.

4. Research the subject.

5. Prepare a tentative curriculum.

6. Propose curriculum to the group (if possible).

7. Set a tentative date, time, and place.

8. Revise curriculum to final (time scheduled) presentation stage.

9. Solicit appropriate instructors.

10. Select and obtain material for programs, participant folders, and instructors (if required).

11. Confirm date, time, and place with all key personnel.

12. One day before the meeting, check equipment availability and readiness of the place for training.

13. Arrive early the day of the seminar to check for unforeseen problems.

14. Present the seminar.

15. Evaluate its effectiveness.

16. Write report on the preparation of and conduct of the training program to document the good points and problems encountered.

17. Send thank-you letters to presenters.

TRAINING AND DEVELOPMENT

perceived as needed by the participants. If the employees see it as a waste of time, not needed, taking them away from their real work, or otherwise non-productive, then very little learning will take place. Management must see that the people selected for the training recognize its importance as much as the company does.

Learning is enhanced through audience participation. By asking questions during the lectures or soliciting comments, the students become a more active part of the learning process. If they are able to learn by doing while in the training program, the potential for learning is greater than if they are just listening.

Feedback during the training also increases learning. Tests, verbal questions, discussions, and other methods that have students presenting or demonstrating what they have learned and receiving feedback reinforces the training goals. Repetition is an important practice to reinforce learning, but too much can be counterproductive.

The training program must be organized in a logical, easily comprehended format. New and complex subjects should be broken down into simple, readily understood steps. The KISS concept should be a byword in program design (Keep It Simple, Stupid).

Materials presented should have real-world applications. First-line supervisors are not that interested in the theories of management of the late 1800s and early 1900s. They want to know how to motivate, lead, and control their workers today. Give the students what they need to succeed in their own work environments, information and skills they can apply when they return to their jobs.

All training should be evaluated to assure that what is being taught is being learned. Post-seminar evaluations by the participants (see Chart 14-4) assist in this area. Student tests also provide information on how well the material has been learned. On-the-job evaluations sometime after the training let the trainers know if the learning has been retained and used, and if not, why not.

This last evaluation is important. If the evaluations during and upon completion of the course show that a high degree of learning took place, but the follow-up evaluation shows that the training is not being utilized, management should be concerned.

Too often companies spend thousands of dollars training their personnel but do not support the application of this acquired knowledge within the organization. In other instances, new management tools are developed at the request of the business. Then, for reasons such as effort required, cost, timing, or management commitment, the new tools were not allowed to be implemented, and the company continues to use the less productive methods.

Not utilizing new or needed skills because they are not working as predicted is one thing; not using these skills because it takes too much time or effort is a cause for inquiry. Follow-up studies can help the trainers and the company recognize where additional obstacles lie or confirm that the training has achieved the desired goals.

STAFFING A SMALL BUSINESS

Chart 14-4 Program Evaluation

Please mark the responses that best express your opinion.

1. The overall program was:

   __ very helpful   __ stimulating   __ too long

   __ interesting   __ too general   __ dull

2. How effective was the presentation?

   __ excellent   __ good   __ fair   __ poor

3. Were you able to hear and understand the speakers?

   __ yes   __ no   Comments: _____

4. How adequate was the material that was presented?

   __ excellent   __ good   __ fair   __ poor

   Comments: _____

5. Was there any subject matter left out of the program that you think should have been included?   __ yes   __ no

   Comments: _____

6. Would you be interested in a program on one specific subject?

   (List) _____

7. How did you learn of this program?

   __ supervisor   __ co-worker   __ company newsletter

   __ other _____ or announcement

8. Why did you attend this program?

   __ supervisor told   __ I asked   __ attendance is
      me to attend   to attend   needed for
                                              promotion

   __ other _____

14 - 10

Chart 14-5 Program Report

Title: Implementation of new travel voucher forms
Date: 16 Oct 1987   Time: 8:00 to 10:00 a.m.
Location: Main conference room
Instructor(s): Ralph Daniels, Accounting Office

Participants: All department secretaries

Number of participants: __8__   Charge cost to: Accounting office

Cost (itemize expenses):
  20 blank forms $6.00 $_____
  Instruction guide $8.00 $_____
  Coffee/juice $5.00 $_____
                            $_____ $_____

                                          Total cost   __$19.00__

Evaluation summary: All participants appreciated formal training in the proper manner to complete and submit the new forms. Participation was active and enthusiastic.

Follow-up: Accounting department will answer any questions regarding new system. No formal follow-up is required.

Problem areas to be resolved: None

STAFFING A SMALL BUSINESS

Chart 14-6 Training Information Sources

Local	High schools Trade or vocational schools Junior colleges Colleges and universities Professional business groups Manufacturers' representatives Local businesses Chambers of commerce City or county government County Extension Service
State	Small Business Development Center (part of the Small Business Administration) State Employment Commission State offices and agencies State certification and licensing boards Professional organizations State universities
Federal	Small Business Administration Service Corps of Retired Executives (SCORE) Active Corps of Executives (ACE) Small Business Institutes (located in college and university business schools) Veterans' Administration Department of Labor Department of Commerce Department of Education Equal Opportunity Employment Commission Occupational Health and Safety Administration
Publication	Training: The Magazine of Human Resource Development Lakewood Publications 50 South 9th Street Minneapolis, MN 55402 612/333-0471

Legal Aspects of Training

Training is usually seen as a means to increase employee skills which should lead to better qualified workers, promotions, and pay raises. Because of these implications, management must ensure that programs do not appear to favor a particular group of employees over others. Non-selection of a person cannot be based on his or her lacking specific qualifications which can be obtained in eight hours of training or less.

Selection procedures for employee training should be based on documented company needs and clear-cut requirements for those personnel who might be eligible. Furthermore, all employees who have satisfactorily completed a training program must have equal opportunities to use their new skills.

When the evaluation of an individual's progress or completion of a training program is used for personnel decision-making, the company must ensure that the evaluator is not biased. An example would be where final grades for a welding school would be used to establish an hourly wage. If male graduates always received higher grades than female graduates, a case for discriminatory practices may be found.

If similar training sessions are conducted for different groups of employees but the training environments are not the same, legal problems may occur. An example could be two groups being trained to use a new computer program. One is being trained in a modern computer lab with the same equipment which will be used on the job; the other is being trained in a noisy, drafty classroom with computers that differ from those to be used on the job. If pay or promotion decisions will be based on the skills acquired from these sessions, one group is at a disadvantage.

In short, training provided by a business must provide equal opportunities to all employees. This does not imply that everyone must be trained to do everything. It does suggest that all people who are qualified to be trained for a position should be considered.

Businesses should keep records of all employees who request company-sponsored training. Documentation on who was selected and how, should be maintained. Management or personnel decisions based on company-sponsored training should be documented. All training records and evaluations on employees who received company-sponsored training should be retained.

Company-sponsored training, like any other benefit, must not become a means for discriminatory practices. Establishing documented needs for company training, offering the training opportunity to all qualified employees, and having a non-discriminatory selection process will go a long way in fending off legal action against a company.

Policies such as those described in Chart 14-7 are other ways to provide company-sponsored educational opportunities to all employees and avoid charges of discrimination.

Getting Your Money's Worth

Losing employees after they are trained is a major concern of employers who pay to upgrade employees' skills. In many instances the fear is justified, a competitor may offer a better deal to a newly trained person than your business does. While it is not possible to guarantee that any employee will remain with a company, there are ways to protect the training investment. If the training is on-the-job, salary increases may be contingent on satisfactory performance resulting from the training.

An example would be a worker who seeks another position but lacks the technical expertise to function in that job. The company agrees to move the person into an OJT position to acquire the skill, then places the person in the new position with increases in pay to be based on satisfactory performance. The trade-off is training now for income increases in the future.

For training that will cost the business money (night school, seminars, and formal training courses), the company may make a loan to the employee to cover the training costs. A schedule can be worked out to permit the employee to reduce the obligation for the loan. For each month the employee remains with the company the loan will be automatically reduced by a scheduled amount.

For example, if an employee needs a $1200, two-month computer training program to move into a new position, the company may give the employee time off with pay to attend the program and may also lend the employee the $1200. The company will reduce the loan by $100 for each month the employee stays with the company upon successfully completing the course. This way the company has the services of the employee for a year or regains part of the training cost if he or she leaves before the year is up.

Some companies encourage employee training by reimbursing school costs when the training is job related. Chart 14-8 describes a policy of reimbursing the employee according to the course grade.

TRAINING AND DEVELOPMENT

Chart 14-7 Example of Employee Training Opportunities

Training and development are continuing day-to-day processes. As such, they are best accomplished on the job, in the environment in which the employee is expected to work. Each department has training requirements unique to its own activities. These may include the learning of a particular system, the operation of a piece of equipment, the training of particular skills. Each department manager is in a position to determine what kind of on-the-job training is desirable. The department manager can then provide the training or make arrangements to have it supplied. Training resources to consider are employees who are technically proficient and vendor representatives and instructors.

From time to time department managers may become aware of professional schools, seminars, or workshops which might be of value to various employees. These may be offered on product changes, maintenance, government regulations, etc. As worthwhile topics appear, employees will be encouraged to attend. Special programs or training will be coordinated with the supervising manager. Expenses incurred by employees while attending approved courses will be paid, partly or in full, by the company. This will be decided by the supervising manager prior to attendance, depending upon the availability of funds and value of the course to the company. Reimbursement may range from paying the employee's salary during the training period to paying salary and expenses.

Department managers are encouraged to develop subordinates for increased responsibilities. Employees who have the capability and potential for advancement are to be considered for promotion as job positions become available within the company. Names of these individuals should be submitted to the supervising manager.

STAFFING A SMALL BUSINESS

Chart 14-8 Example of Reimbursement Policy

The company encourages employees to improve their technical and intellectual skills by pursuing and successfully completing appropriate courses of study. The company will share in the cost of after-work courses, provided successful completion will improve the employee's competence and value to the company.

The company does not reimburse tuition for technical courses taken by an employee to fulfill the minimum work standards required in order to perform his or her job.

The company's procedure for tuition reimbursement is as follows. Before enrolling in a class, an employee must submit information on course content to the department manager and supervising manager. A copy of the class training schedule or course catalog should provide the information needed. Course approval is made by the supervising manager and placed in the employee's personnel file. Tuition fees are refunded after the class is completed based on course grade.

    Course grade: A = 100% tuition reimbursement
                   B = 75%
                   C = 50%
                   D = 25%
                   F = no reimbursement

When requesting tuition reimbursement, an employee must submit his or her paid tuition receipt and final grade report to the department manager. Approval for payment will be made by the supervising manager.

TRAINING AND DEVELOPMENT

Worksheet 14-1 Training Needs Evaluation Form

Employee: Date:

Position: Department:

Supervisor:

EX = Excellent
AA = Above Average
 A = Average
BA = Below Average
UN = Unsatisfactory

Skill Level

Skill area:	EX	AA	A	BA	UN
Ability to					
Ability to					
Ability to					
Ability to					
Ability to					
Ability to					
Ability to					
Ability to					
Ability to					

Supervisor's comments:

Supervisor's recommendations:

Supervisor: Date:

STAFFING A SMALL BUSINESS

Worksheet 14-2 Program Report

Title:
Date: Time:
Location:
Instructor(s):

Participants:

Number of participants: _____   Charge cost to: _____

Cost (itemize expenses):

        _____ $_____
        _____ $_____
        _____ $_____
        _____ $_____

                          Total cost _____

Evaluation summary:

Follow-up:

Problem areas to be resolved:

Chapter 15
Alternative Ways to Staff a Small Business

Summary of Chapter

Alternative ways of handling the staffing needs of small businesses have evolved over time. These include contracting work to independent agents, using temporary employees from an agency, and leasing employees from a company that supplies the business' entire work force.

Each alternative provides the business with workers from an outside source. The company management directs the daily and long-term operation of the organization but is not responsible for payroll or personnel matters.

Personnel costs are commonly 20 to 40 percent above a company's actual payroll. The reporting and recordkeeping requirements are detailed and time-consuming. A company may incur a single set cost for its personnel through a negotiated contract. This single charge per employee covers salary and benefits, and eliminates almost all personnel paperwork requirements.

Temporary Help Agencies

Temporary help agencies specialize in "renting out" employees to fill a particular short-term need in a company for whatever length of time is required: from four hours (the usual minimum work period) to as long as several years. The types of employees available cover a wide array including clerical workers of all skill levels, light and heavy industrial workers, medical support personnel, technicians, marketing specialists, computer operators, and maintenance and janitorial employees.

Filling an employment need quickly is one advantage temporary help agencies have for companies. They have rosters of workers on call who are available for temporary assignment. Personnel can often be supplied within thirty minutes after the request has been received.

Temporary help agencies are bonded; they are licensed by the state and must operate under state guidelines. Requirements may vary, but this normally includes Workers' Compensation and unemployment insurance on the agency's employees, and liability insurance coverage.

STAFFING A SMALL BUSINESS

Employers are generally billed weekly. The agency takes care of all worker records, compensation, and support paperwork. Cost to the employer for a temporary employee cannot be calculated by any set formula. The agency fee would include the amount paid to the worker, a percentage to cover the administrative costs plus a mark-up (commonly based on supply and demand) for that job in that particular locale.

The 1984 Tax Act amended the definition of a leased employee. Some temporary employees who perform full-time temporary services for the same business for over a year may now be classified as leased employees. This may affect the contractual relationship regardingpay and benefits.

The principal advantage to using temporary personnel is the availability of skilled workers on short notice to fill a designated need.

Contract Workers

Contracting work to independent individuals is another alternative to increasing a company's work force. In this instance, a contractual arrangement is made for the work project itself to be handled outside the organization. A company may elect to contract out for a variety of reasons including short-term or one-time assignments, when business is cyclical or seasonal, when specialized skills are needed but not on a permanent basis, when direct control is not a requirement, when agencies do not offer the necessary skills or when it is not feasible to take on the project internally.

Employer-employee relationships are defined and explained under the Fair Labor Standards Act (see Chapter 5). The courts interpret an employer as one who has the authority to hire and fire, provides immediate supervision or control of work and services, must pay for the work performed, and has the power to establish the wage and hours of employment.

Common law (law decided by judges) has established basic classifications of employees, one of which is an independent contractor. An independent contractor relationship occurs when the employer does not have the right to control the means by which the work is performed. The employer retains the right to accept or reject the finished product. The primary element in establishing an independent contractor relationship is not what it is called in a contract, but the substance of the contractual relationship.

Obviously a contractual agreement may contain gray areas. A husband-wife home-based business may want to contract out 40 hours of typing. If they provide the typewriter, the office space to be used, and they only want the typing done during the week between 9 a.m. and 5 p.m., the IRS may question whether the typist is truly an independent contractor. On the other hand, if the rough drafts are given to a typist who does the work elsewhere with specific instructions regarding the format of the finished product and when it was to be returned, this should qualify as work by an independent contractor.

ALTERNATIVE WAYS TO STAFF A SMALL BUSINESS

Before using contract services, the company should obtain legal guidance on any liability it might incur when the contract is fulfilled or expires. The guidance should apply to IRS regulations and to any legal obligations relative to the contract workers. In some instances the contract worker has filed for unemployment compensation after completing the contracted work and been able to collect, with the company having to pay the compensation benefits.

Employee Leasing

In employee leasing or contract staffing a business relinquishes all personnel and payroll activities to an outside firm. Under this system, the business acquires its employees from an independent leasing company.

At the outset, it should be understood that employee leasing is a relatively new concept. The regulations and guidelines that cover employee lease companies vary from state to state. Before undertaking this type of arrangement, company management should contact the office of the state controller or attorney general to learn what controls, if any, the state has regarding this service.

In many instances the employee leasing process starts out with the employer business terminating its staff, who are then hired by the outside company and leased back to the employer. Employee leasing offers several benefits to both the employees and the owners. For the employees, a larger and more comprehensive benefit package is a part of their employment with the leasing company, their legal employer.

Assuming the leasing company has contracts with many small businesses, its numbers of employees (actually the workers of several small businesses) would allow participation in a wide variety of comprehensive benefit plans such as medical, pension, and education. The leasing company would enjoy lower costs for these benefits.

Another advantage for the leased employees is greater job mobility. If an employee leasing company contracts with many small businesses, openings in one client firm could be filled by a leased employee working for another firm. This way there would be no disruption in company benefits.

There are also many advantages to the owners of the small business. Participation in the program allows them to be competitive with larger companies when seeking new employees who place a value on company benefits. For this reason employee leasing programs have been very attractive to small professional businesses such as medical clinics, dental offices, law firms, and other professional organizations that only need one or two clerical, administrative, or reception personnel. A leased employee, as defined by Congress, is one who essentially works on a full-time basis for at least 12 months.

Another advantage is in the form of a tax shelter for a small business. The 1982 Tax Equity and Fiscal Responsibility Act (TEFRA) prohibits employers from establishing a better pension plan for themselves than their workers. In a

STAFFING A SMALL BUSINESS

business with no employees (other than the owners), up to $100,000 annually may go inito the owner's own pension plan. Thus, taxable net income may be contributed directly into the pension plan, escaping immediate corporate or personal taxation. A leased employee, as defined by Congress is one who essentially works in a full-time basis for at least 12 months.

A third major advantage is the obvious release from paperwork. The administration and legal requirements incumbent on an employer are now passed on to the employee leasing company. The former employer still retains the workers but has almost no responsibility regarding record keeping or personnel administration.

An obvious question the small business owner has is "What will this cost?" If all costs relative to staffing an organization were calculated (costs not only for the pay and benefits, but also for bookkeeping, maintaining records and files, heat, electricity, office space, etc.), then the leasing expense probably would not cost that much more. While several of these separate costs may be insignificant to a business (extra file drawers, one-eighth of a bookkeeper's time, etc.) the main attraction for the owner is being released from the personnel function responsibilities.

The leasing company can make its profit two ways. First is by adding a service fee charge or percentage to the costs incurred by them. Second is to be able to run a more efficient personnel operation and take advantage of group discounts on benefit plans. Operating the personnel functions for 200 small businesses in actuality can be the same as for one large business.

Typically the leasing company will provide gross salary, social security contribution, unemployment, required disability insurance, workers compensation, and employee benefits. The cost of leasing an employee can range from 125% to 142% of the employee's gross pay. This charge would include a 5% to 10% administrative fee (based on the employee's gross salary).

The IRS has become concerned that employee leasing companies are not what they claim, but are instead false set-ups to avoid taxation. The employee leasing company must adhere to the common law regulations pertaining to employer-employee relationships; it must provide the actual supervision for the employee's work and provide performance appraisals, pay adjustments, and legal benefits.

The business continues to manage the day-to-day and long-term operation of the organization, but all personnel functions are the responsibility of the leasing firm. Payroll records; federal, state and local reporting forms and supporting records; Workers' Compensation and unemployment claims; insurance and benefit packages; and the activities related to hiring, counseling, and firing are commonly handled by the leasing firm.

Under this system, a liaison is assigned to the business to coordinate the various personnel functions and to see that the personnel goals of both the employee leasing company and the business are met. The liaison's role is to serve as the link to insure that the contract is carried out satisfactorily and in accordance with all applicable laws.

ALTERNATIVE WAYS TO STAFF A SMALL BUSINESS

The business organization functions in much the same way as it did before the leasing arrangement. Performance reviews are done according to the established timetable with the added involvement of the field supervisor in the review process.

The employee leasing company is responsible for hiring and firing decisions, but the business leasing the workers retains considerable influence because the staff must be able to perform the work. The business retains the right to determine job requirements and staffing needs.

Before any business decides to enter into contract staffing, it should seek professional counsel as to the ramifications of this process and obtain a clear understanding of how it works and how it may affect employer-staff relationships. Additional information on employee leasing may be obtained from the National Association of Contract Staffing Agencies, 4870 Haygood Road, Virginia Beach, Virginia 23455, 804/499-6863.

Conclusion

The personnel functions of a business can be a very complex aspect of management. Federal and state laws are constantly changing and court interpretations add to the confusion. Staffing a Small Business is guide to assist owners and managers to function effectively and legally when hiring, compensating and evaluating their employees.

Many of the forms found in an employee personnel file document unique relationships or contracts between that employee and the business. The charts and worksheets in this book are designed to serve as guides for developing those forms you specifically need for your business. Because of the tremendous variability in jobs, size of businesses, and services or goods produced, few forms are applicable to all businesses without change.

The information provided in this book should assist owners and managers to better understand the staffing aspects of their business and aid in creating the personnel forms needed.

The Successful Business Library

*A Company Policy and Personnel Workbook	$33.95
Career Builder	$33.95
Controlling Your Company's Freight Costs	$33.95
Cost-Effective Market Analysis	$33.95
Debt Collection: Successful Strategies for the Small Business	$33.95
*Develop Your Business Plan	$33.95
The Loan Package	$33.95
Mail Order Legal Manual	$45.00
Managing People	$33.95
Marketing Your Products and Services Successfully	$33.95
Negotiating the Purchase or Sale of a Business	$33.95
Preventing Crime in Small Business	$33.95
Proposal Development: A Winning Approach	$33.95
Publicity and Public Relations Guide for Business	$33.95
Risk Analysis: How to Reduce Insurance Costs	$33.95
Surviving and Prospering in a Business Partnership	$33.95
Staffing a Small Business: Hiring, Compensating and Evaluating	$33.95
*Starting and Operating a Business in...(See list of states on other side)	$29.95
Tax Tips for Small Business, 1989	$12.95
Venture Capital Proposal Package	$33.95
*Corporation Startup Package & Minute Books	$33.95

California   Colorado   Florida   Texas

Software

PSI Research has a number of easy-to-use software programs, most of which are compatible with the Successful Business Library books (See titles with asterisks).

Formats are available for IBM and compatibles or Macintosh.

Other titles include

- CPR - Customer Profile & Retrieval — Customer Database. No other program needed. Automatically sorts customers by name, company, city, and zip code ... $69.95

- Financial Management for Small Business
  Basic skills for financial analysis and planning—Excel (Macintosh)
  Book and disk ... $69.95

For more software product information, please call PSI Research.

PSI RESEARCH/THE OASIS PRESS
300 North Valley Drive
Grants Pass, OR 97526
(503/479-9464)
(FAX 503/476-1479)

The Successful Business Library

*Starting and Operating a Business in . . . .

California
Colorado
Florida
New York
Texas
Washington

Author Michael D. Jenkins and co-authors (most of whom are associated with the accounting firm of Arthur Young and Company) have put together a step-by-step manual which guides you through federal and state laws and regulations. A "one-stop" resource guide.
$29.95 each

Alabama	Iowa	Nebraska	Pennsylvania
Arizona	Kansas	Nevada	S. Carolina
Arkansas	Kentucky	N. Hampshire	Tennessee
Connecticut	Louisiana	New Jersey	Utah
Delaware	Maryland	New Mexico	Virginia
Georgia	Massachusetts	N. Carolina	W. Virginia
Hawaii	Michigan	Ohio	Wisconsin
Illinois	Minnesota	Oklahoma	Wyoming
Indiana	Missouri	Oregon	

Also Available in 1989 (Please call for availability dates) . . . .

Alaska	Maine	North Dakota	South Dakota
Dist. of Col.	Mississippi	Rhode Island	Vermont
Idaho	Montana		

Title	Price	Qty	Total
_____	____	____	____
_____	____	____	____
_____	____	____	____
_____	____	____	____
		Subtotal	____
		Total	____

The Oasis Press
Toll-free order phone
1-800-228-2275

__ Check enclosed (payable to PSI Research (shipping free via UPS within the continental U.S.)

__ Charge (shipping added) to __ VISA __ Mastercard __ American Express

Card # _____ Expires _____/_____/

Name as shown on card _____

Signature _____

(We ship via UPS so please give a street address rather than a P.O. box)

Ship to _____ Title _____

Company _____

Address _____

City _____ State _____ Zip _____

PSI RESEARCH/THE OASIS PRESS
300 North Valley Drive
Grants Pass, OR 97526
(503/479-9464)
(FAX 503/476-1479)